The Vikings: A Very Short Introduction

VERY SHORT INTRODUCTIONS are for anyone wanting a stimulating and accessible way in to a new subject. They are written by experts, and have been published in more than 25 languages worldwide.

The series began in 1995, and now represents a wide variety of topics in history, philosophy, religion, science, and the humanities. Over the next few years it will grow to a library of around 200 volumes – a Very Short Introduction to everything from ancient Egypt and Indian philosophy to conceptual art and cosmology.

Very Short Introductions available now:

ANARCHISM   Colin Ward
ANCIENT EGYPT   Ian Shaw
ANCIENT PHILOSOPHY
   Julia Annas
ANCIENT WARFARE
   Harry Sidebottom
THE ANGLO-SAXON AGE
   John Blair
ANIMAL RIGHTS   David DeGrazia
ARCHAEOLOGY   Paul Bahn
ARCHITECTURE
   Andrew Ballantyne
ARISTOTLE   Jonathan Barnes
ART HISTORY   Dana Arnold
ART THEORY   Cynthia Freeland
THE HISTORY OF
   ASTRONOMY   Michael Hoskin
ATHEISM   Julian Baggini
AUGUSTINE   Henry Chadwick
BARTHES   Jonathan Culler
THE BIBLE   John Riches
BRITISH POLITICS
   Anthony Wright
BUDDHA   Michael Carrithers
BUDDHISM   Damien Keown
BUDDHIST ETHICS   Damien Keown
CAPITALISM   James Fulcher
THE CELTS   Barry Cunliffe
CHOICE THEORY
   Michael Allingham
CHRISTIAN ART   Beth Williamson

CHRISTIANITY   Linda Woodhead
CLASSICS   Mary Beard and
   John Henderson
CLAUSEWITZ   Michael Howard
THE COLD WAR   Robert McMahon
CONSCIOUSNESS   Susan Blackmore
CONTINENTAL PHILOSOPHY
   Simon Critchley
COSMOLOGY   Peter Coles
CRYPTOGRAPHY
   Fred Piper and Sean Murphy
DADA AND SURREALISM
   David Hopkins
DARWIN   Jonathan Howard
DEMOCRACY   Bernard Crick
DESCARTES   Tom Sorell
DESIGN   John Heskett
DINOSAURS   David Norman
DREAMING   J. Allan Hobson
DRUGS   Leslie Iversen
THE EARTH   Martin Redfern
EGYPTIAN MYTH   Geraldine Pinch
EIGHTEENTH-CENTURY
   BRITAIN   Paul Langford
THE ELEMENTS   Philip Ball
EMOTION   Dylan Evans
EMPIRE   Stephen Howe
ENGELS   Terrell Carver
ETHICS   Simon Blackburn
THE EUROPEAN UNION
   John Pinder

Available soon:

For more information visit our web site

www.oup.co.uk/vsi/

Julian D. Richards

THE VIKINGS

A Very Short Introduction

OXFORD
UNIVERSITY PRESS

OXFORD
UNIVERSITY PRESS

Great Clarendon Street, Oxford OX2 6DP

Oxford University Press is a department of the University of Oxford.
It furthers the University's objective of excellence in research, scholarship,
and education by publishing worldwide in

Oxford New York

Auckland Cape Town Dar es Salaam Hong Kong Karachi
Kuala Lumpur Madrid Melbourne Mexico City Nairobi
New Delhi Shanghai Taipei Toronto

With offices in

Argentina Austria Brazil Chile Czech Republic France Greece
Guatemala Hungary Italy Japan Poland Portugal Singapore
South Korea Switzerland Thailand Turkey Ukraine Vietnam

Oxford is a registered trade mark of Oxford University Press
in the UK and in certain other countries

Published in the United States
by Oxford University Press Inc., New York

© Julian D. Richards 2005

British Library Cataloguing in Publication Data
Data available

Library of Congress Cataloging in Publication Data
Data available

ISBN 978-0-19-280607-9

3 5 7 9 10 8 6 4

Typeset by RefineCatch Ltd, Bungay, Suffolk
Printed in Italy by
Legoprint S.p.A., Lavis (TN)

Contents

List of illustrations

The publisher and the author apologize for any errors or omissions in the above list. If contacted they will be pleased to rectify these at the earliest opportunity.

Chapter 1
Vikings then and now

Every February the schoolchildren of York dress up in traditional Viking costume and this northern English city holds its annual Jorvik Viking Festival. Sagas are retold, battles are re-enacted, and Viking longships race along the River Ouse. The rape and pillage has been toned down and York's modern traders have embraced Vikings with more enthusiasm than their 9th-century forebears: at the time of writing, shoppers at the out-of-town designer outlet can design a Viking tunic, Viking-related books are on display in Borders and Waterstones, *The Vikings* starring Kirk Douglas and Tony Curtis is being shown at the local cinema, and cafes and snack-bars offer a variety of longboat baguettes and Viking-themed sandwiches. The festival promoters claim that the event harks back to Jolablot, a midwinter festival held by 'the original Vikings', although in fact it was invented in 1985, and marks the annual downturn in visitor figures to Jorvik, the Viking-themed tourist attraction.

It is hard to escape Vikings in York. Although the city's visible heritage owes more to its Roman, Norman, and medieval builders, opening a telephone directory reveals a host of Viking enterprises – Jorvic Business Systems, Jorvik Cleaning Services, Yorvik Homes & Developments Ltd, Yorvik Shipping, Yorvik Refrigeration, and the ominous Viking School of Motoring – to name but a few. Clearly Vikings have a contemporary resonance –

and not just in York. Similar reinventions can be found in the Isle of Man, the Northern and Western Isles, in Normandy and Brittany, across the Atlantic to North America, and in Scandinavia itself.

But 'Viking' is a nebulous concept – in different contexts Vikings have been marauders, merchants, manufacturers, poets, explorers, democrats, statesmen, or warriors. It is also a relatively recent concept – originally used to refer only to pirate activity, it came to be used as an ethnic term to refer to a whole people, and then as a chronological label, giving its name to the Viking Age. With this fluidity it did not mean the same in 10th-century Scandinavia, 15th-century Iceland, and 19th-century England. In fact, our modern usage of Viking owes more to later reinventions than any original reality.

This book will attempt to deconstruct the term, but will also seek to demonstrate why it has retained its importance. Focusing particularly on archaeological discoveries of the last 30 years, it will examine what is actually known about the peoples who lived in Scandinavia in the 9th and 10th centuries, the areas they colonized, and their relevance today.

Who, what, and when were the Vikings?

The term *viking* was first used in Old English. It occurs just three times in the Anglo-Saxon Chronicle where it refers to 'robbers', apparently coastal marauders rather than land-borne armies. It was not used in other countries which suffered raids from Scandinavia, and Western observers gave the raiders many different names. In some cases it was their religion, or lack of it, that was significant, and they were referred to as pagans, heathen, or gentiles. In the Irish Annals they were often seen as just different and were called *gaill*, or 'foreigners'. In other contexts it was where they came from that was of interest, and they were *Northmanni*, or *Dani*, although such labels were often used indiscriminately, irrespective of their

1. Red Erik: Danish luxury beer

actual area of origin. Finally, it may have been their function that stood out, as *pirate* or *scipmen*.

At first, the Scandinavians thought of themselves as inhabitants of particular regions, such as men of Jutland, Vestfold, Hordaland, and so on. Their loyalty would have been to their leaders, rather than to any national identity. Their armies comprised warriors from different parts of Scandinavia, and they were the followers of Olaf, Svein, Thorkel, or Cnut. Nonetheless, they did speak the same language, which linguists have called Old Norse, and shared aspects of a common culture, including costume, art, and religion. As a sense of national identity grew so did the use of national names. In time, Dane was used to describe southern Scandinavians whilst Norse was used to describe those from northern areas.

The specific root *viking* reappears in the 11th century in Old Norse, with a different emphasis. In the elegy *Knutsdrapa* Cnut's troops are called *víkingar* to emphasize their ferocity, and the same word appears on 11th-century rune stones to describe respectable sons raiding overseas as well as local nuisances. By the 13th century it was used in Icelandic Sagas to refer to pirates, but it was not generally used in Western European sources during the Middle Ages. In Scandinavia it only came into common usage during the rise of 19th-century nationalist movements. It is recorded in modern English for the first time in 1807–8, and was revived by Sir Walter Scott in 1828 in *The Pirate*.

The actual derivation of the term *viking* has been much debated. It has been suggested that both the Old English and Old Norse forms are parallel developments from a common Germanic verb meaning 'to withdraw, leave or depart'; that it is related to the Old Icelandic *vik*, meaning a bay or creek; that it refers to those from the area of *Vik* or *Viken* around the Oslofjord who embarked on the raiding of England to escape Danish hegemony; that it derives from *vika*, a turn on duty, or relay oarsmen; that it derives from an Old Icelandic verb *vikya*, meaning 'to turn aside', or the Old English *wic*, or armed camp.

Whatever the derivation, it is clear that the majority of Scandinavians were not Vikings; only those who went 'a viking' should really qualify for the description. It would be perverse, however, to abandon the term at this point, although this book will generally try to restrict its usage to describe those involved in raiding or other warlike activities, and to those instances where the Viking stereotype has been reused in a more recent context, either as an adjective or as a noun. At other times the less loaded term Scandinavian will be used and, following common practice, Norse will be used for those peoples of Scandinavian culture in the North

Atlantic, without necessarily assuming that they came from Norway. In other cases, the more accurate terms Hiberno-Norse, or Anglo-Scandinavian will be used, reflecting the fact that it is frequently a hybrid identity that is being described.

The chronological term 'Age of the Vikings' followed the classification of Ages of Stone, Bronze, and Iron, and was first invented in Scandinavia to label cases of artefacts in the National Museum in Copenhagen in the 1840s. It was taken up in du Chaillu's *The Age of the Vikings* (1889) and later by Peter Sawyer in *The Age of the Vikings* (1962). In the hands of some authors and coffee-table books it has turned Viking identity into a stage on an evolutionary ladder, a super-identity, and a great civilization, analogous to the Ages of Greece or Rome. However, no one can agree when it was.

The start of the Viking Age can no longer be fixed categorically at 793 with the raid on Lindisfarne because there is evidence of earlier contact, in the form of Irish and English artefacts in 8th-century Norwegian graves. Whether loot or traded goods, these indicate early North Sea crossings. The inhabitants of Sweden had also engaged in earlier expansion in the Baltic, and in southern Scandinavia many of those characteristics that have been associated with the 'Viking Age' begin to emerge during the early 8th century. They include the development of towns, the centralization of authority, a shift from exchange to market-based trade, increased production, and overseas contact. The dispute is really between those who see raiding as the key characteristic of Viking activity, and are reluctant to place that earlier than the 790s, and those who see outward-looking expansion, state formation, and other positive features taking place from the 710s.

Raiding activity intensified in Western Europe from the 830s and a Viking camp was established in Dublin in 841. There were attacks on Frankia and Spain in the 850s and raids and then settlement in Russia from the 860s. From the late 870s Vikings settled permanently in England, and also founded colonies in the Isle of Man, the Northern and Western Isles, the Faroes, and Iceland. Greenland was settled in the 980s and around 1000 there were voyages to Vinland and North America. However, fixing a date for the end of the Viking Age is also problematic. It has often been linked with particular events in the English calendar, either when Harthacnut, the last Scandinavian king of England, died in 1042, or when Haraldr Hardrada was defeated at Stamford Bridge, in 1066. However, Scandinavian presence continued in Scotland, Ireland, and the Isle of Man beyond that, although aggressive military activity had stopped by the second half of the 11th century. Scandinavian culture also continued in the North Atlantic, and in Iceland and Greenland into the 14th and 15th centuries, and some of these areas have retained a Viking cultural identity to the present day.

Since this book is about this nebulous concept of Vikings, it will embrace all these areas and periods. It will be concerned not just with how Viking identity has been redefined in medieval and modern times, but also with how cultural identities were formed and negotiated in the 8th–12th centuries, in a variety of geographical contexts.

The approach taken has not been to present a strict chronological history of the Vikings. Instead a more geographically-based approach has been adopted, starting with Scandinavia, and working outwards, but using each chapter to develop a specific theme. Chapter 2 looks at where the Vikings originated and Chapter 3 considers their ideology and religion. Chapters 4 and 5 then present the evidence for increasing settlement complexity – both rural and urban – and the growth of the nation states. Chapter 6 examines the evidence for their sea-faring prowess and begins to consider Scandinavian expansion overseas, starting with Western Europe and Russia. Subsequent chapters then provide a series of case studies, beginning with England in Chapter 7, and then looking at the Irish Sea region in Chapter 8, the Northern and Western Isles in

Chapter 9, the North Atlantic in Chapter 10, and culminating in Greenland and North America in Chapter 11. An attempt has been made to introduce the key evidence from these areas, focusing especially on the latest archaeological discoveries. A secondary aim has been to use each case study to examine the complex relationship between colonists and colonized in a number of environments, and to consider the present-day relevance of that relationship. Chapter 12 emphasizes the ways in which our views of peoples in the past are shaped by the present by looking at the reinvention and reuse of Vikings in a variety of 19th- and 20th-century contexts.

Ethnic groups used to be regarded as cultural and biological isolates, but now we understand that cultures only exist in relation to other cultures, and that they define themselves in terms of their differences, or similarities, with other societies. People use language, costume, architecture, religion, and burial practices to create identities, and in colonial contexts they can adopt a number of strategies – of isolation, hybridity, assimiliation, or genocide – to negotiate their position in relation to indigenous societies in new environments. Was there such a thing as a contemporary Viking identity, or was it created in a variety of guises – as Anglo-Scandinavian, Hiberno-Norse, Icelander, or Rus – in response to different local situations? There are important messages for modern Europe here. To find out more, read on.

Chapter 2
Early Scandinavian kingdoms

To understand the Viking Age it is necessary to start with Scandinavia, and to examine the changes that were taking place there from at least the 8th century onwards. By considering Scandinavian culture and society at home it should also be possible to see how it spread and how it was adapted and assimilated in Scandinavian colonies overseas.

Scandinavia first appears in Pliny the Elder's *Naturalis historia* (d. AD 79), where it is a 'dangerous land on the water'. Today, it comprises Denmark, Norway, and Sweden, and is generally seen as including Finland, although the Finns are a different language group. It is especially the Danes, Norwegians, and Swedes who trace their national origins to the Viking Age. Scandinavia covers 12 per cent of the total European landmass, but its population makes up only 3 per cent of the European total, and the great expanses of the interior have always been sparsely populated. The population of Scandinavia even today is little more than 17 million: Denmark has the highest density with 5 million, followed by Sweden with 8 million, and Norway with 4 million. In the Viking Age the relative distribution was probably much the same, although the density was lower, with extensive settlements throughout southern Sweden except where there were thick forests, Norway except where it was mountainous, and Denmark except for the sandy moors of Jutland.

The modern Scandinavian countries did not exist at the start of the Viking Age. Whereas the kingdoms of Anglo-Saxon England and Continental Europe had accepted the Christian view of the King as God's prime servant on earth, this was not the case in Scandinavia. Scandinavian societies maintained their old structure of tribes, each dominated by a numerous aristocracy, and temporarily ruled by a chieftain.

By the 10th century, Scandinavian warlords who had spent time in Europe returned home and tried to foster new ideas. People were Christianized and royal authority was established. By the 12th century the aristocracy managed to convert power based on old ideologies into new power structures, defined by privileges, documents, and laws. By 1200 each Scandinavian country was established as a nation state according to the Western European pattern.

The Viking Age is therefore seen as the period during which these countries acquired their national identities, and since there is very little written documentation, the dating of archaeological evidence for these early state societies has considerable significance. In recent years a lively debate has waged amongst Scandinavian archaeologists on the subject of the processes that led, during the Scandinavian Iron Age and Viking Age, to state formation. We will examine this evidence, including the increasingly complex hierarchy of rural settlements and the emergence of towns, but first we need some geography.

Denmark took its name from its people, the Danes, although the meaning of the suffix -*mark* is unclear. Today, Denmark comprises the Jutland peninsula, the large islands of Fyn and Sjælland, as well as 500 smaller islands, and the island of Bornholm in the Baltic. However, during the Viking Age it also included Skåne, Halland, and Blekinge, which were ceded to Sweden in 1658. Its southern frontier lay at the foot of the Jutland peninsula, in what is now north Germany. During the Viking Age much of Denmark was extensively wooded with oak and beech, although there were also sand dunes and heath. Nowhere was more than 55 kilometres from the sea, which provided the basis of livelihood. Cultural innovations reached Jutland first; it is not surprising that it became the main centre of royal power when Denmark emerged as a unified state in the 10th century.

In his *History of the Franks*, Gregory of Tours (538/9–94) reported that in 515 a Danish fleet under a King Chlochillaich invaded Gaul from the sea. It is not known where the Danes referred to came from, or how large an area their king ruled, nor indeed what sort of power he exercised there, although Gregory explicitly uses the term *rex* for the Danish king. Further 6th-century sources mention the

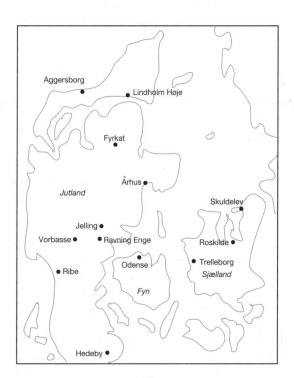

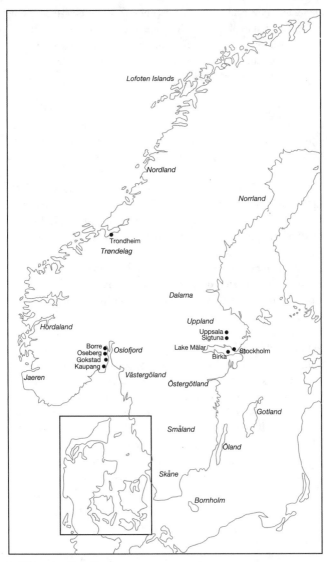

2. Viking Age Scandinavia

Danes as a powerful force and Procopius (c.500–c.565) tells of how the Heruli had to pass through the territory of the Danoi on their way to Scandinavia. But care is required in interpreting such reports; we should not impose either later medieval or Roman concepts of 'kings' or 'peoples' onto other situations.

Scandinavia was outside the Roman Empire, although Roman influence reached Jutland and is reflected in prestigious diplomatic gifts in Danish Iron Age graves. Such objects were designed to secure frontier zones; they appear to have consolidated the power of local chiefs, empowering them within a gift exchange economy, and maybe establishing power relationships which continued into the Viking Age. The chiefs were not at the pinnacle of the gift exchange for it was their role to officiate over gifts to the gods. The gifts also need to be set against a background of an ideology based upon warfare, in which the spoils of war were given as offerings to the gods in great bog deposits, such as those excavated at Illerup and Ejsbøl in Jutland. Hoards were a particular element in the establishment and legitimation of the elite, which communicated with the gods on behalf of the community.

In the 7th and 8th centuries there are only scattered references to Danes and their kings in contemporary sources. We know, however, that the missionary Willibrord, bishop of Utrecht, visited King Ongendus, who ruled over 'the wild tribes of the Danes', within the period 690–714. Only at the end of the 8th century and particularly in the first half of the 9th century do Frankish Annals provide fuller information on Danish kings, who emerge as worthy opponents of Charlemagne and his successors. We are given the names of a number of kings, including Godfred, and get the impression of a kingdom that already included Skåne and the area around the Oslofjord.

There is archaeological evidence for an organized central power in Jutland in the 8th century. The island of Samsø had strategic importance in the seas to the east of Jutland, and at Kanhave a timber-lined canal, 500 metres long by 11 metres wide, linked the sea to the west of the island with a protected bay to the east. The Kanhave canal would have allowed ships with a draught of up to 1.25 metres to pass from the naval harbour to the west. Tree ring dating shows that the canal was constructed in 726, repaired *c.*750, and could have remained in use until 885.

At the foot of the Jutland peninsula there was the Danevirke, a system of fortifications 14 kilometres long, closing the Schleswig pass between the Schlei fjord which cuts in from the east, and the marshy areas around the rivers which flow into the North Sea on the west. The first ramparts were constructed in 737, and extended under King Godfred in 808. The Danevirke is unlikely to have been purely a mechanism for defence; it was probably as important in controlling the movement of people and animals. It would be a mistake, however, to take these isolated instances of monumental construction under royal authority as evidence for an 8th-century state that corresponded to modern Denmark.

The name Denmark is first used by Wulfstan, archbishop of York (931–56) and it occurs again later in the 10th century, on the two royal rune stones at Jelling. From the mid-10th century we know of a continuous succession of kings, beginning with Gorm the Old. Royal power was extended under his son Harald Bluetooth, who conquered Norway in the early 960s; Harold was ousted in 987. Gorm's grandson, Svein Forkbeard, and his great-grandson, Cnut, both led armies against England, the latter becoming king in 1016–35. By the late 10th and 11th centuries there was regular Anglo-Danish contact and the exchange of craftsmen between England and Denmark.

Harald Bluetooth (d. *c*.987)

Harald Bluetooth was the son of King Gorm, father of Svein Forkbeard, and grandfather of Cnut. His name – Blåtand in Old Norse – probably means dark complexion. In an early rune stone, erected at Jelling, in central Jutland, *c*.960, Harald claims that he unified Denmark and Norway and converted the Danes. There are also two massive burial mounds at Jelling. Apart from a silver goblet, the northern burials had been removed, but excavations in Jelling church in the 1970s located a 10th-century chamber containing a disarticulated male skeleton. It is now believed that the northern mound was erected by Harald *c*.959, as a memorial to his parents, along with the rune stone. After his conversion he had them removed to the church, and also erected the southern mound, which became a cenotaph memorial to himself.

Harald is credited with several massive public works, which should be viewed in the context of Danish conflict with the German Emperor. In 968 he linked the Danevirke to Hedeby and also extended and rebuilt it with a timber rampart. In 979–80 he built a large bridge over the Vejle river valley at Ravning Enge. The roadway was 720 metres long and 5.5 metres wide; it was supported by more than 1,500 oak timbers and must have been intended as a military road.

In the 980s he built a series of circular fortresses at strategic locations throughout his kingdom – they are named after the example at Trelleborg in Sjælland, but there are other examples at Fyrkat in central Jutland, Nonnebakken on Fyn, and an unfinished one at Aggersborg from the tip of northern Jutland.

Each of the forts was constructed to a regular geometric blueprint. They had circular ramparts of earth and turf, surrounded by a V-shaped ditch, and covered gateways at all four compass points. The gates were linked by timber-paved streets, and by another road inside the rampart. In each quadrant bow-shaped halls were arranged around a quadrangle. Only a quarter of the halls were lived in although, at both Trelleborg and Fyrkat, cemeteries have been found outside the ramparts. The forts must have represented regional centres for the royal power of Harald Bluetooth, however, they were only used for around ten years, and only that on Fyn became a major town. They seem to have been a reckless expense, each one containing at least 16 fantastic halls with convex walls, porches, and end rooms, yet were used as storerooms and workshops, and monuments to Bluetooth's vanity!

Norway took its name from the sheltered sea route down its western coast, the *Norvegur*, or 'North Way'. The coastline is indented by countless fjords; measured in a direct line it is 3000 kilometres, but its real length is 20,000 kilometres. Mountains arise directly from the western coast and the Viking Age population was confined to narrow ledges and small plains at the heads of the fjords, where communities developed in relative isolation, each with its own traditions and culture. More than half the country lies at altitudes above 600 metres, but there are just a few fertile areas of gentle slopes where population is concentrated: Jaeren, in the south-west, Oslofjord, in the south-east, and Trondelag in the north-east. Even today agricultural land accounts for only 3 per cent of the surface area; forests make up 23 per cent and here there was iron, and unlimited supplies of wood, as well as wild animals, including deer, elk,

3. Rune stone, Jelling. The inscription reads: 'King Harald had this monument made in memory of Gorm, his father, and Thyra, his mother. That was the Harald who won all of Denmark for himself, and Norway, and made the Danes Christian.'

4. Artist's impression of the fortress at Fyrkat; one of the four quadrants has not been excavated

wolf, bear, and fox. The northern coastal strip of Halgoland was thinly populated; here the Norse took tribute from the Saami. The sea was a major resource, with whale, seals, and walrus in the far north.

Norway was first unified in the 880s by Haraldr Finehair, king of Vestfold which included southern Norway and the coastal districts, but not the far north. Haraldr died *c.*930 and was succeeded by his son, the infamous Erik Bloodaxe (p. 70). Norway shared a border with Sweden and also a short stretch with Denmark but difficulties of land communication meant that the population looked naturally to the sea, and to opportunities in the west. The first recorded Viking raiders in the British Isles were probably from Hordaland, in western Norway, and the Norse were the main Scandinavian colonists in the Northern and Western Isles, the Faroes, Iceland, and Greenland.

Sweden takes its name from the Svear people of central Sweden. Its modern boundaries incorporate a varied landscape with wide variations in soil, climate, and relief. To the north of Skåne, the low plateau of Småland was sparsely populated, and in the Viking Age provided a natural border with Denmark. Beyond, the central lowlands were divided into two well-forested and fertile regions: the Svear, centred on Uppland, and the Gotar, to the east of Vanar. Further to the north, Norrland comprised forest and bare rock and was again sparsely populated. In the Baltic, the islands of Gotland and Öland had good farming land and were of particular strategic importance in the Viking Age. Southern Sweden had a coastal climate; the north had very cold winters with much ice and snow. Coniferous forest still covers 57 per cent of the landmass; it provided opportunities for hunting and fishing in the Viking Age.

International trade was developed in the Baltic, with links south to Byzantium. Swedish Vikings tended to look eastwards, although several joined expeditions to the west, to England and Normandy. Throughout the 9th century several kings are mentioned in Birka, but the extent of their control is unknown. Sweden was only unified in the course of the 11th and 12th centuries, as a result of a lengthy power struggle between Östergötland and Västergötland.

In northern Sweden and Norway, Norse societies came into contact with the Saami peoples, although they have been excluded from most histories of the Viking Age. In the 19th century, whereas the study of Vikings emerged as an historical discipline, tracing the roots and lineage of a people through their folklore, myths, and national history, the Saami were given an ethnography, and studied as foreign and primitive hunter-gatherers. From the late 1970s, however, Saami academics and intellectuals began to reclaim their culture, and a younger generation of Scandinavian historians and archaeologists also began to observe symbiotic interaction between Norse and Saami culture. Burial data has been used to extend the mobile range of the Saami far to the south of their modern boundaries during the Viking Age; birch bark burials in the pre-Viking cemeteries at Vendel and Valsgärde in Uppland have been taken as evidence for a Saami presence, and dietary evidence has suggested a reliance on reindeer far south of their natural habitat. Immigration of 'non-Western peoples' is a big political issue in modern Scandinavia and archaeological evidence has been used to demonstrate that during the Viking Age large areas of Scandinavia supported two ethnically distinct population groups who lived side by side.

To an extent, therefore, Scandinavia has always been on the fringes of Europe, not just geographically, but culturally as well. Despite regional differences, the Scandinavian peoples were united by proximity to the sea, and this has helped foster a sense of transnational identity. This emerged for the first time during the Viking Age. In the next chapters we will explore the ways in which a Viking cultural identity has been defined.

Chapter 3
Pagans and Christians

The Viking stereotype rests upon aggressive paganism. Viking raiders who attacked undefended monasteries have been accused of doing so not just because these sites represented easy sources of wealth, but explicitly because they were Christian. 'Paganism' is itself often used as a pejorative term and is generally avoided in this book. Recent approaches have examined the nature of pre-Christian belief systems and their borrowings from other religions. Conversion is no longer seen as a one-off act of enlightenment, although contemporary Scandinavian kings liked to portray it as such. Instead it is understood as a gradual process in which Christianity coexisted alongside older beliefs in an early medieval multi-faith society.

Aspects of Viking ideology may also be found in art. In 21st-century Western society we generally distinguish between applied art and pure art, and artistic endeavour is separated off from the everyday world. In modern terms all Viking art was applied art, and has sometimes been regarded as the decoration of functional objects. However, was Viking Age decoration purely functional or did it have an ideological component? How valid is this distinction between pure and applied in other cultures?

The evolution of Scandinavian-style animal ornament has often been treated as a typological device which can help in the dating of objects, and in mapping the spread of Viking society and culture. It has been taken as evidence of civilization, and an indication that despite all that rape and pillage the Vikings had good taste. More recently some archaeologists such as Bjorn Myhre have begun to see art styles in terms of ethnic symbols and identities that were used in a deliberate expression of Vikingness. Others have focused on the possible ideological meaning of the motifs. Animal ornament may represent part of a totemic belief system, for example. It is important not to forget, however, that our knowledge of Viking art is generally dependent upon durable objects of metal and stone; wood and textiles are rarely preserved; human skin, which may have been elaborately tattooed, has never survived.

Pre-Christian belief systems

To us 'religion' conjures up a set of beliefs and rules of behaviour that embody concepts of worship, with holy men or women to interpret them. In Scandinavia before Christianity, however, no one would have understood this. It is probably more appropriate to talk about a 'belief system', a way of looking at the world. Religion was just another aspect of life and the act of worship as required by the Norse pantheon was not adoration or even uncritical approval, and therefore it was utterly unlike the Christian relationship with the divine. According to Norse mythology, everything ended at Ragnarok, when all humans and gods were killed and burnt. According to this philosophy the outcome of our actions is predetermined, and we cannot change our fate; what is important is our conduct as we go to meet it.

Vikings had a more fluid sense of the boundaries between this world and the next, as well as between the world of humans and the world of beasts. Under Norse mythology there were many classes of supernatural beings. There were two families of gods: the Æsir, including Oðinn and Thor; and the Vanir, including Njord, Freyr and Freyja. However, there were also servants of the gods, such as the valkyries, and Oðinn's raven, as well as giants, dwarves, elves, trolls, spirits, ghosts, and so on. Sorcery, and the practice of *seiðr*, was fundamental to Viking beliefs. Neil Price has suggested that *seiðr* was the Norse counterpart of shamanism, and that comparable features can be seen amongst the Saami, from whom some of its features may have been borrowed. Specific grave-goods, such as metal and wooden staffs, silver amulets shaped like chairs and animal masks, may indicate the burials of practitioners.

A grave in the cemetery at the Danish ring fort at Fyrkat has been interpreted as the burial of a witch or sorceress. A wagon was used as a coffin for the woman's body. She was not buried with the customary pair of brooches but was wearing two silver toe rings, and was accompanied by a Gotlandic box brooch. It has been suggested that she came from the Baltic region. Her grave-goods included a bronze bowl containing fruit, two drinking horns, an iron spit, and traces of a wooden staff. There were also several amulets, including a silver chair, a sheepskin pouch (probably containing henbane seeds), and a drinking glass. By her feet was a locked oak box, containing clothes, a pair of shears, a slate whetstone, a pottery spindle whorl, the lower jaw of a young pig, and a clump of owl pellets.

Two women were laid out in the burial chamber within the Oseberg ship (p. 48): one aged *c.*25, and the other aged *c.*50. The younger woman may have been a princess and the older one her slave, but other objects in the grave also indicate at least two roles: that of princess and that of high priestess, roles which may have been combined in one person. Two small tapestries depict processional scenes with imagery of Freyja and Oðinn and some of the grave-goods suggest that the tapestries depict real events rather than just myth. They included an oak chest which contained a sorcerer's staff and two iron lamps which resemble those being carried in procession, as well as five wooden animal heads, and a cart carved with images of cats, the sacred animal of Freyja.

There seems to have been no single pre-Christian burial rite and there was tremendous regional variation throughout Scandinavia. Nevertheless, widespread practice was to bury the dead fully clothed with personal adornments, together with a selection of implements and utensils of everyday life, whether the rite chosen was cremation or inhumation. The intention appears to have been to equip the dead for the next world, which was imagined as being very like this. Oðinn needed slain warriors to be buried with their weaponry, and the wealthy were accompanied by their horses, dogs, and slaves. Burial with boats, wagons, or horses represented the journey into the next life, and if a whole boat was not available a stone setting in the outline of a ship might do.

In much of Norway and Eastern and Central Sweden cremation was the most common form of burial, but it was rare in Denmark, outside northern Jutland. In Sweden cremation was prevalent during the preceding Vendel period and continued, with boat burial, into the Viking Age. Cremation graves under mounds generally cluster around farms. Cremated remains could be placed directly into a pit, put into a bag or a pottery or metal vessel, or spread

5. Burial mounds, Birka

upon the ground. Multiple cremations are known. In southern and central Jutland and northern Norway inhumation was prevalent from the beginning of the Viking Age. The body might be placed directly into the ground, or in a coffin, chamber, or vehicle. Contrary to popular belief the majority of burials were poorly furnished. Ninth-century burials are the simplest and the knife was the most common simple find, in graves of both sexes. A distinctive group of rich 'cavalry' burials with weaponry and equestrian equipment appeared in Denmark in the 10th century. Grave-goods are sometimes included in Swedish graves up until the 12th century.

Temples and cult places

The majority of pre-Christian religious activity probably took place in open spaces and sacred groves. The so-called pagan temple at Old Uppsala referred to by Adam of Bremen has been reinterpreted as a large feasting hall in which pagan festivals may have taken place at certain times, rather than a dedicated religious building, although the use of the place-name element *hof*, as at Hofstaðir in Iceland, may indicate the use of a building for religious rituals.

During the 1980s a number of new structures were found which support the idea of small-scale, local, religious and votive activities carried out at special sites. Excavations on the highest point of the island of Frösön – literally Freyr's Island – in Sweden, under the floor of a medieval church, uncovered what appear to be the remains of a sacrificial grove. Under the medieval altar were the decayed remains of a birch tree, which had been deliberately felled. Around its roots was a large animal bone assemblage which had accumulated while the tree was standing. This included the whole bodies of five bears, the heads of six elks and two stags, as well as remains of sheep, pigs, and cows. These may have been skins or whole bodies which had been hung from the tree. Radiocarbon dates place the activity in the 10th and 11th centuries; the stone church was built towards the end of the 12th century.

At Borg, in Östergötland in Sweden, a cult building was attached to a chieftain's farmstead. The building came into use as early as the start of the 8th century although most of the ritual activity belonged to the 10th century. It comprised two rooms separated by a passage; along the eastern wall there was a stone platform, possibly a plinth, on which idols were set. Two rings were found in the south-west part of house, but there were no other finds. The surrounding ground surface was covered with large stone paving, and the overlying layer contained a hoard of another 98 rings, as well as 75 kg of unburnt animal bones and slag. The rings appear to have been used to carry amulets, such as hammers or axes, which are usually found singly in graves. Some were unfinished, suggesting they were being manufactured here. Three adjacent buildings with sand floors had been used for metalworking.

The animal bones comprised unusual proportions of jaws and skulls, perhaps remaining from sacrificial meals, as well as a large number of horses, at least ten dogs, plus pups and some wolves. There were smaller numbers of cats, beavers, badgers, foxes, red deer, and geese, as well as the more usual domestic species. The sow and boar bones had been spatially separated: the boars (possibly representing Freyr, male god of lust and sexuality) with the furnace; the sows (possibly representing Freyja, his female counterpart) with the amulet rings. In the 11th century the cult building was demolished and the area covered with a thick layer of gravel; a stone church was built 100m east of the cult area in the 13th century, but may have been preceded by a wooden church.

Conversion and Christianization

Given the differences between Scandinavian belief systems and Christian religion it appears that conversion was as much a process of developing new approaches to ideology as dealing with a clash of religions. Traditionally, conversion took place under royal direction, first in Denmark (under Harald Bluetooth in 965), and later in Norway (under Olaf Tryggvason in 995) and finally in Sweden (under Olof Skötkonung, in 1008). However, research has indicated that Christianization was a long process stretching over several centuries preceding its official ratification, and that it may have proceeded in parallel in each of Scandinavian countries, albeit with regional differences.

The initial contact was probably the result of early Christian missions. In the early 8th century, Willibrord, an English monk working in Frisia, extended his mission to the Danes. He probably sailed to Ribe where, according to Alcuin, he was welcomed at the court of King Ongendus, but making little progress he gave up and sailed back to Frisia with 30 boys.

It was recorded in Rimbert's *Vita Anskarii*, or 'Life of Ansgar', that in 829 a king of the Svear, in eastern Sweden, asked the Frankish Emperor, Louis the Pious, for a missionary to visit his country as many wanted to adopt the Christian faith. Two monks from the monastery of Corvey, Ansgar and Witmar, were appointed to the journey to Birka. They converted Herigar, described as a prefect of Birka, and some years later a church was built, although there was a revolt in 847 which led to suspension of pastoral activities until 854. Ansgar then re-established the mission and received permission to build churches and appoint priests. Ansgar died in 865 but, according to Adam of Bremen, a new mission was launched in 936. Unni, archbishop of Hamburg-Bremen, visited Gorm and his son Bluetooth, and also travelled to Birka, where he died. Unni's successor, Adaldag, consecrated bishops for Hedeby, Ribe, and Århus in or before 948.

Christian objects, many found in Scandinavian graves, have often been regarded as loot, but it has been suggested that some at least may represent early missionary activity. These include over 30 cross- or crucifix-shaped pendants, five 8th- and 9th-century crosiers (from Hedeby, Lund, Helgö, Stavanger, and Setnes), six reliquaries, and some 15 Frisian or Tating-ware jugs. These vessels were frequently decorated with silver-foil crosses and they have been associated with the Christian liturgy, possibly being used for storing and measuring liturgical wine. Five such jugs were found in 9th-century graves from Birka; one was found with an Irish hanging bowl with fish-shaped mounts in the grave of a woman laid out east–west and whose grave-goods also included two cross-shaped rectangular brooches.

Women played an important role in pre-Christian Scandinavian religion, but it has been argued that conversion was a disaster for women. There was no Christian goddess, and religious practice was officiated over by men. Anne-Sofie Gräslund and others have rejected this, arguing that the exclusion of women only comes later, and that women played an important role in the Christianization of Scandinavia. Some aspects of Christianity would have been attractive to them, including the prohibition of infanticide, the equality of the sexes before God, and belief in a paradise from which women were not excluded, unlike Valhalla. The majority of the pendant crosses and Tating-ware jugs come from female graves and women had a key role in dedicating rune stones (see below).

Christianization is generally visible in the burial record. Christian burials may still have contained dress items, but there was a decrease in grave-goods. A rich 10th-century Danish grave recovered from Mammen in 1868 is characteristic of the transition to Christianity. The grave-goods included a gaming board and a famous silver-inlaid axe but there were no other weapons, and a large candle had been placed in the chamber. Tree ring dating of the burial chamber places it in 970–1, just five to ten years after the conversion of the royal Jellinge dynasty.

Cremation was prohibited by the early church as a pagan practice and declined during the 10th century, although in some areas it continued to be practised. At Valsta, in the Uppland region of Sweden, there is a typical farm cemetery of the Mälaren valley comprising c.70 burials, the majority dating to c.800–1150. During the 9th and 10th centuries all graves were cremations, and there is no indication of any Christian influence from Birka, although the grave-goods indicate broad contacts including a glass beaker, Frankish, Frisian, and Slavonic pottery, Arabic coins and weights, and continental sword types.

Around 950 the inhumation rite was introduced, but cremation continued to be used in parallel until at least the mid-12th century. The inhumations may represent the introduction of Christian beliefs, and although they are orientated east–west, they also still contain pagan elements, including grave-goods, Thor's hammer amulets, and food offerings. Around 1100 a third group of graves was established on the northern plateau at the top of the cemetery. Secondary inhumations were inserted into a large mid-9th-century barrow by removing a 6m-diameter area from the centre of the barrow and inserting three cist burials. The earlier cremation layer was placed around the insertions and a kerbstone added to the mound. Unfortunately all three cist burials were later robbed, but a small iron cross was recovered, as well as a rock crystal and white quartz beads. The symbolic placement of the burials indicates a strong identification with the earlier chiefly burial, but also clear Christian symbolism coexisting with 12th-century cremation.

The 10th-century introduction of monumental rune stones provided a new means of commemoration of the dead. There are 2,500 Viking Age runic inscriptions in Sweden, *c.*250 in Denmark (including southern Sweden), and *c.*65 in Norway. The densest distribution is in the Uppland region of central Sweden, with 1,300 rune stones, over 60 per cent of which date to the establishment of a diocese there in the late 11th century. Birgit Sawyer has argued that rune stones had a secular function in ensuring inheritance and marking individual claims to land and this is certainly true, but the vast majority of rune stones are also Christian monuments. Over half are decorated with a cross, and over 200 contain prayers in the form of 'May God help his/her soul . . . ' Several rune stones mention the conversion of whole regions (p. 16). The early church incorporated bridge building into a system of indulgences, comparable to the giving of alms or going on a pilgrimage. Around 150 rune stones were erected as monuments close to bridges; of these it is notable that 55 per cent were erected by women.

The dating of the rune stones emphasizes that Christianization was a long-drawn-out process. Although it is believed that Ansgar established a church in Birka in the 9th century, the earliest churches found archaeologically belong to late 10th and 11th centuries. Following a pattern seen slightly earlier in England, many rural churches in southern Scandinavia appear to have started life as private estate chapels built of timber in the 10th century, followed by a documented explosion of stone church building in the 12th and 13th centuries. In some cases there is extraordinary evidence for continuity of sacred places. At Mære, for example, in the Trøndelag district of mid Norway the present stone church was built *c*.1150–1200. It was preceded by a wooden 11th-century church, which itself overlay Christian burials suggesting a still earlier church. The first church lay on top of a cultural layer with four post-holes and 19 gold foils, maybe the location of the high seat of a 9th-century hall or *hof* site.

In conclusion, although 'pagan' practices and belief systems have become an essential part of the modern definition of Vikings, for 9th-century Scandinavians pre-Christian beliefs provided just another aspect of life. These beliefs were not exclusive and early Scandinavian kings soon embraced Christianity as another means by which they could legitimize their rule. In later chapters we shall see, however, that in some situations Scandinavian colonists overseas used burial rites as a means by which they could maintain a distinct identity, in the face of indigenous pressure to assimilate. First, we need to examine changes in Scandinavian rural settlement.

Chapter 4
Changes in the countryside

Archaeologists studying the development of early states in Scandinavia during the Viking Age have argued that their origins lay in social and economic processes already under way in the late Iron Age. Major excavations in advance of development, as well as the archaeological recording of metal-detected finds, particularly in southern Scandinavia, have revealed a process of gradual settlement evolution, as well as a growing complexity of settlement types.

In Norway and the Swedish interior a pattern of isolated farmsteads, with small clusters of dwellings and outbuildings, was established during the Iron Age. In Denmark and southern Sweden there were relatively mobile villages as well as individual farms before the 9th century, but there is evidence for new patterns of landholding during the 10th and 11th centuries, and the establishment of the modern settlement pattern by the 12th century, reflected in place names ending in *-toft*, *-torp*, or *-by*.

Denmark and southern Sweden

In Denmark the period 500–800 was once seen as a period of decline, but more recent excavations show this was a prosperous age with growing social stratification; they demonstrate that the apparent desertion of settlements actually represents localized settlement movement. Archaeological work and metal detecting has also revealed a much more complex system of settlement hierarchies.

Throughout southern Scandinavia a number of more specialized sites begin to emerge from the 6th century. Some appear to have functioned as production sites and landing places, established by aristocratic families who were looking for the opportunity to exchange production surplus for prestige goods. Many also incorporated religious functions. They include sites such as Helgö in Uppland; Paviken in Gotland; Gudme, Strandy Gammeltoft, and Fyn's Hoved in Fyn; Boeslunde, Vester Egesborg, and Næs in Sjælland; Sebbersund and Bejsebakken in northern Jutland.

At Gudme, in South-East Fyn, an Iron Age settlement complex of over 50 farms covered a square kilometre. Over 7,000 metal objects dated 200–1000 have been found within the settlement area, including six gold and five silver hoards, testament to the power base of the local aristocracy. Many of the farms belonged to craftsmen, on which goldsmiths and silversmiths worked, and where bronze casting was carried out. The main building was an imposing late Iron Age hall – an aristocratic residence whose inhabitants drank from Roman glasses and ate from Roman bowls. The adjacent coastal trading site at Lundeborg acted as the port of trade. Gudme also had some cult function; the place name means literally 'home of the gods'. Although it declined from the 6th century, its trading and manufacturing functions continued into the Viking Age.

A similar site existed at Uppåkra in Skåne. This also developed as a central place in the Iron Age, but maintained trading, manufacturing, and religious functions until *c*.1000, when it was superseded by the town of Lund, 5 kilometres to the north. Metal objects have been found over a 40-hectare area, including Arabic and Carolingian coins, tiny gold foil votive mounts or *guldgubber*, dies for their manufacture, and miniature amulets.

The site at Næs was occupied from the late 7th to 9th centuries. There were over 20 timber halls, but also some 70 workshops which must have been used as spinning and weaving sheds as each contained loom weights and spindle whorls. In a low-lying part of the site there were also 57 wicker-lined pits, used for retting flax. A 150-metre long channel had been dug to facilitate changing the water. Antlers were also found in several of the pits where they were being soaked prior to being worked. At Sebbersund there is evidence for a zoned trading and manufacturing centre comprising over 300 workshops, where weaving and ferrous and non-ferrous metal-working took place.

Vorbasse, in Jutland, was the first site where a sufficiently large area was examined to demonstrate a process of localized settlement movement, culminating in the establishment of a permanent village towards the end of the Viking Age. From 1974–92 over 260,000 square metres were excavated, revealing at least eight separate settlement shifts between the 1st century BC and the 11th century AD, as part of a process of local migration and rebuilding to make the most of the agricultural land. By the 8th century there were seven enclosed farms of roughly equal size, either side of a roadway. Each farm had a main hall, partitioned into rooms, and frequently with byres at one end. The halls were surrounded by workshops; some had wells, and one had a smithy.

The fact that the number of farms at Vorbasse did not change for 300 years has been taken as evidence that the inhabitants were not free and independent landowners but must have been tenants of a magnate farmer or local lord who regulated the farms directly or through a steward. In the late 10th or early 11th centuries there was a major change in building style and the main buildings were replaced by large bow-sided halls, of the type seen at the Trelleborg forts. Separate cattle byres were constructed – the largest farm had five byres with room for at least 100 cattle, as well as a forge and a bronze foundry. In the 11th century the settlement moved for the last time, to the site of the present village.

Although the excavations have been smaller in scale, a similar situation – including the appearance of bow-sided halls – has been observed at other sites in Jutland, such as Sædding, Trabjerg, and Omgård, and in Skåne, at Filborna, where several generations of aisled longhouses were succeeded by 'trelleborg'-style houses in the 11th century. At Lindholm Høje, in northern Jutland, the bow-sided halls of the 11th-century village were built upon windblown sand which had covered the cemetery of the older settlement. In turn they were themselves covered by sand by the 12th century.

This process of mobile settlements being replaced by permanent villages was repeated throughout northern Europe at the onset of the Middle Ages. Various reasons have been proposed, including population pressure limiting settlement movement and leading to the demarcation of territorial boundaries. The development of villages goes hand-in-hand with the formation of parishes and the construction of permanent stone churches, but it is also related to the growth of cereal production and wealth being vested in land ownership rather than mobile resources such as cattle. Alongside this was the growth of royal control, with the attendant requirement on stable settlement to ensure a stable tax revenue. Although it is impossible on the basis of archaeological evidence alone to demonstrate the origins of a feudal system in Denmark during the Viking Age, it is at least reasonable to talk about the development of lordship and landholding on behalf of superior authority.

Several settlements reflect the growing concentration of power from the 7th century, and Viking Age aristocratic residences at Toftegård (Sjælland), and at Slöinge (West Halland) develop from earlier settlements. In both cases the high-status objects were concentrated in the hall areas.

At Tissø, western Sjælland, an exceptional settlement has been discovered on the shores of Lake Tissø, 7 kilometres from the coast, and accessible from the sea via river. The site has been investigated by metal-detector survey, and excavation since 1995. The first phase of activity is represented by a large aisled hall with white plastered internal walls dated to the 6th–7th centuries. This hall was set in an enclosure with two other large houses and a few smaller buildings and workshops. It burnt down in the mid-7th century and was replaced by a substantial bow-sided hall on a new site to the south. This structure was unusual in that there was no stalling for cattle, and although a forge was built by the enclosure fence, there was no trace of any agricultural buildings. In the 8th century the hall was rebuilt, the enclosure extended, and a wide gate was built in the enclosure fence to enable wagon access. The main hall was rebuilt a second time in the 9th century, at the same time as the enclosure was further enlarged. The complex reached its maximum extent in the 10th century. A large hall of the new 'trelleborg' type was erected, in addition to several other dwellings, and open-ended buildings, possibly wagon sheds, although there was still no trace of agricultural production. In 1977 a 1.8 kg gold neck ring of the 10th century was found by metal detector. This would have been a tremendously precious object, equivalent in value to 500 cattle, and the type of gift that might have been given by a king to a loyal follower; it later turned out to have been hidden just outside the gate of the residence. The latest find from Tissø was a coin of King Harthacnut, *c.*1035.

Tissø was not an agricultural estate – there are few stalls for cattle and it must have been supplied with food by dependent farms in the area. Its economic base depended upon tribute, trade, and manufacture. Outside the manor enclosure, to both north and south, there was a 2–3 hectare workshop and market area with around 70 sunken workshops and also small houses or booths in which goods may have been traded under the lord's protection. Here goldsmiths and silversmiths worked, and bronze was cast into costume brooches, while other craftsmen made glass and amber beads and combs. Over 100 coins have been found, dating from a late 7th-century sceat, and including 8th-century Scandinavian and Frankish coins, although most are 9th- and 10th-century Arab issues; their distribution suggests trading was taking place on site.

A mid-9th-century Byzantine lead seal, bearing the name of Theodosius, is identical to examples from Hedeby and Ribe. Theodosius was head of the Byzantine armoury and recruiting office; Lars Jørgensen has suggested that he may have been buying iron or recruiting mercenaries in northern Germany and Denmark.

Tissø may be an example of an aristocratic or even royal residence. Weapons and riding gear, including spurs, bridles, and a large number of arrowheads and sword mounts are concentrated in the enclosure area. Frankish and Carolingian drinking vessels were also found in the area around the central halls. Miniature amulets, including Thor's hammers, fire steels, and tiny lances have also been recovered from this part of the site, possibly associated with an enclosed votive area. Tissø means 'Tyr's Island' and was named after the war god Tyr. Some 50 swords, axes, and lances were found on the lakebed in the 19th century. They go back to *c.*600, around the date of the founding of the settlement, although they continue into the 9th and 10th centuries, and probably represent offerings to Tyr. Tissø demonstrates that Viking Age lords had several functions: they were responsible for military protection of the local area, they controlled trade and crafts in the marketplace, and they were responsible for heathen cult ceremonies, including feasting in the great hall.

Finally, at Old Lejre, near Roskilde (Sjælland), excavations have examined the mythical seat of the Danish kings. From the 7th to the 10th centuries the settlement comprised two functional areas: a residential complex of 50 houses, including four halls, each *c.*48 metres long, and a craft area consisting of workshops and smaller buildings. Over 4,000 finds were recovered, including gilt jewellery, casket fittings, coins, weights, silver and bronze ingots, moulds, riding equipment, imported jewellery, mounts, and glass of Carolingian and Anglo-Saxon origin. The fact that the settlement remained in the same place for *c.*300 years is unusual and Lejre has also been seen as a royal residence.

Norway

In Denmark and continental Europe the extensive and continuous areas of cultivated land made it possible for the aristocracy to restructure their landed estates. In northern Scandinavia natural features such as marshes, forests, rivers, and valleys made the running of large estates difficult. It was more efficient to maintain small farms as individual units and so the basic settlement structure in Norway remained unchanged from the 6th century. In southern Norway and along the Atlantic coastline as far north as Tromsø there were chieftains who operated within a redistributive economy, passing prestige goods to their followers in return for food rent. In the Jaeren district of southern Norway the available land was cultivated intensively and Bjorn Myhre has argued that territories or chiefdoms, centred upon hillforts, emerged from around the 6th century, when they can be recognized from their rich graves. The building types continue with little change from the Iron Age into the Viking Age. Farms consisted of small clusters of aisled longhouses, combining living accommodation for an extended family and a cattle byre under one roof.

In northern Norway this mixed farming economy coexisted with a different cultural tradition, associated with the Saami, which depended upon hunting in the inner fjords, interior, and far north. This society is seen as mobile and egalitarian, although it was ignored in the Norwegian literature until the 1980s in favour of what was seen as a more Viking way of life. In the border area around the Lyngen fjord there are Norse burials to the south and Saami burials to north, although some intermarriage at elite level may be suggested by Saami jewellery in Norse high-status burials in this area. There is also a concentration of hoards containing Norse and Saami objects in the border area which may represent gift exchange used in the negotiation of the frontier zone. The collapse of the chieftain system and the end of pre-Christian religion may have led to much tenser relations with the Saami.

Excavations at Borg in Norway have revealed traces of a Viking chieftain's lifestyle maintained for at least 300 years. The Lofoten Islands lie above the Arctic Circle, in the most northerly region settled by Scandinavians; the distance from Borg to the southern border of Denmark is as great as from there to Rome!

The original timber and sod-walled longhouse was built in the 5th–6th centuries, but during the 7th century this was extended and replaced by a second aisled hall, *c*.80 metres long by 7.5–9 metres wide. The hall was divided into three aisles by two rows of timber posts which supported the roof; it had five rooms and five entrances. The hall continued in use for some 300 years; by the time it was demolished it must have been a very old-fashioned building, although its long life and traditional architecture may have signalled the long continuity of the ruling family.

Despite its northerly location the climate was ameliorated by the Gulf Stream, and everyday life revolved around cattle, reflected by a substantial byre, although barley was also grown. Sinkers and fishhooks demonstrate that fishing was also a significant component of activity, and the stockfish trade was no doubt important. Large quantities of iron slag were found and forging may have been undertaken in a smithy, although iron was imported from southern Norway. Soapstone was also imported and various artefacts were manufactured here: spindle whorls, drilling weights, net sinkers, and loom weights. Multicoloured pendant whetstones, of a type known from Hedeby, were also produced. Other finds included sherds of two Tating-ware jugs and 12–13 glass vessels of the 8th–10th centuries, some decorated with applied gold foil, which link the owner to the ceremonial drinking tradition of the north European elite. The imported goods represent symbols of power and prestige; similar imported objects have been found only at Kaupang in Norway. Parallels have been drawn between Borg and Ohthere's account of *c*.890. No doubt he visited the feasting hall, although it has been concluded that this farm belonged to another chieftain, named Tore Hjort. Ruins of large boathouses show the chieftain certainly possessed boats capable of sailing the same distances as Ohthere. The economic basis may have been similar, although no walrus bones found, and there were no artefactual links with the Saami.

Ohthere

Ohthere, or Ottar, was a Norwegian merchant who visited King Ælfred in the late 9th century. Although we do not know what language they spoke, or whether they used an interpreter, Ælfred asked Ohthere about his lifestyle and travels, and had them recorded in English.

Ohthere's homeland was in the far north of Norway, above the Arctic Circle, and his farm may have resembled that excavated at Borg. His land was poor and much of Ohthere's income came from exploiting the reindeer. He also went whaling and walrus-hunting, and took tribute from the neighbouring Lapps. This was in kind (presumably walrus ivory and furs) and so Ohthere had his own ship and travelled south to the markets of Northern Europe.

Ohthere told Ælfred that no one lived north of him but that there was a market town to the south called *Sciringesheal* (Kaupang). He said that it took at least a month to get there under sail if you laid up at night and had a favourable wind every day. All the time you must sail along the coast. From Kaupang he said he sailed five days to the trading town at Hedeby.

In the 10th–11th centuries the chieftain's residence was succeeded by three much smaller buildings which seem to reflect a more typical farmstead. This may indicate a dramatic change in local power politics, associated with the rise of royal Norwegian power. The pattern is similar to the end of the aristocratic central places and settlement disruption seen in southern Scandinavia.

Borg was a religious centre both in pagan and Christian times. The central room in the hall appears to have been used for feasting, cult ceremonies, and festivities. The majority of the imported objects, including fragments of a hanging bowl, five *guldgubber*, and the head of a gold manuscript pointer were found in the northern corner of this room, which may represent the position of the high-seat. The hall may therefore have been used as a pagan temple or *hof* on special occasions, the local chieftain combining sacred and secular roles. Although continuity of ritual practice cannot be demonstrated it may be significant that the parish church is still situated at Borg.

Throughout Scandinavia, therefore, there were major changes in rural settlement patterns during the Viking Age, reflecting growing social complexity and increasing hierarchies and specialization of site function. There is nothing intrinsically Viking about these developments, and similar changes were taking place elsewhere in Europe. Nonetheless, they did underpin the establishment of the Scandinavian nation states and provided the basis for overseas expansion. At the upper end of the settlement hierarchy a new type of site emerged: the town. This is the subject of the next chapter.

Chapter 5
Towns and trade

Although the early medieval period was a time of urban regeneration and rebirth throughout much of Northern Europe, the growth of towns in Viking Age Scandinavia has had a particular role in changing the popular image of Vikings, and emphasizing their identity as traders and manufacturers. Earlier research, inspired by the Belgian historian Henri Pirenne (1862–1935), saw towns as the result of economic development, particularly long-distance trade, but they have now come to be regarded as the product of local power structures. The foundation of urban markets and international trading ports has been seen as intrinsically linked to the growth of royal power and the establishment of the early Scandinavian states. With this has grown a competition to find the earliest town and recent excavations have seen the dates for sites with urban features being pushed further and further back into the Iron Age. Most of the early evidence comes from present-day Denmark and northern Germany, southern Sweden, and southern Norway. There are large areas of Scandinavia where there were no towns until the later Middle Ages.

We have already seen that from the 6th century a number of early trading and manufacturing centres were established around the southern Scandinavian coastline. These are not towns as such, but have been classed as proto-urban centres. Although the definition of towns has been much debated by medieval historians and archaeologists, urbanism is above all a concept underpinned by some level of town planning and control.

One of the earliest Scandinavian towns was founded at Ribe in southern Jutland, *c*.704–10. Excavations have revealed a network of regular plots, surrounded by wattle fences and separated by small ditches. These plots were laid out from when the first merchants arrived, and have been taken as direct evidence for royal patronage and organization, although the thick layer of sand once thought to have been deliberately laid to level the site has now been reinterpreted as a windblown deposit. Eric Christiansen has argued against the tendency to ascribe Ribe to state action, and has suggested that it depended upon cooperation amongst merchants while the king merely tried to stay in control of the situation.

As no traces have been found of solid buildings, but only of semi-sunken huts and workshops, Ribe may have been a seasonal periodic market and manufacturing centre rather than a permanent residence. Specialized metal workers were casting a range of jewellery types, while others were making glass beads, using tessarae imported from northern Italy. There were also imported quern stones and pottery from the Rhineland and, from the 8th century, the minting of a silver *sceatta* coinage in the so-called Woden monster type. From the early 9th century Eidsborg slate whetstones and soapstone bowls were imported from Norway. Many of these goods were dispersed to the hinterland, and imported finds have been recorded from over 30 local sites. In return cattle were brought into Ribe for consumption and possibly export; thick layers of cattle manure have been found. By the mid-9th century Ribe was surrounded by a town ditch. However, as this was only 2 metres wide by 1 metre deep it cannot have had a defensive function and appears, instead, to have denoted a mercantile zone, possibly under royal protection and tax jurisdiction.

The Swedish kingdom began to develop in the 7th century around the great lakes of Central Sweden and the earliest town was at Birka, situated on the island of Björkö in Lake Mälaren, and 12 kilometres east of the proto-urban production centre at Helgö. On the island of Adelsö, on the other side of the strait, stand the remains of a royal manor. It is tempting to see this as the power base from which Birka was controlled and taxed, albeit from a distance. The first excavations on Björkö were carried out in the 1680s, and while Hjalmar Stolpe's excavations from 1871–90 yielded vast numbers of imported finds, the full sequence of Birka's development has had to await recent investigation.

Birka was fortified, on land and water, from its foundation in the mid-8th century. The first town was enclosed by a semi-circular rampart, divided into seven segments by six openings, which were probably gated, and presumably guarded by towers. At its northern end the rampart extended out into the harbour in Lake Mälaren as a series of piles. Adjacent to the rampart, excavation has revealed terraces upon which houses predating the town had been built. Finds from a longhouse of c.400–700 show far-reaching trade contacts before the town was established.

The town was also protected by a small fort – the 'Borg' – enclosed by an earth and stone bank with a wooden rampart. The presence of rivets suggests it was constructed using boat-building techniques, or using lots of ships' timbers. The Borg was first fortified c.750 when the town was founded, but it was burnt down in the 9th century, rebuilt and raised in height but fired again in the late 10th and 11th centuries. Beneath the hillfort is an area known as the garrison because of the number of weapon finds. Stone terraces had been built on sloping ground between two rock outcrops. The upper terrace was covered by a substantial 10th-century hall, which appears to have functioned as an assembly hall for the permanent garrison. Three pairs of stout roof-bearing posts created a large open space in the middle of the building. From within the hall the finds included armour and chain mail, shields, and spears which stood against the walls; swords, arrowheads, axes, horse fittings, and locks and keys indicating the presence of chests. The finds' distribution suggests the presence of a high seat in the western part of hall. The garrison had direct access to the shore, and must have been situated to protect Birka from attack from the seaward side. Two jetties of oak piles are visible just below the area of the garrison, indicating a military harbour kept separate from the commercial one. Birka also had several cemeteries, and Stolpe excavated 1,100 burials, including 119 rich chamber graves. They represent a cosmopolitan mercantile community with wide-ranging trading contacts. Unlike Ribe, Birka appears to have been permanently occupied from the start. The number of times it was attacked, as well as the steps taken to defend it, is perhaps significant.

The town of *Reric* is mentioned in the Royal Frankish Annals in connection with King Godfred's activities in the early 9th century. It is probably to be associated with the site at Groβ Strömkendorf, on the shores of the Baltic. In the 1990s 258 burials were excavated, displaying a variety of Saxon, Frisian, and Slavonic cultural influences, and including six Scandinavian boat graves. The settlement is dominated by semi-sunken workshops, and an impressive series of timber-lined wells which may have been used for dying textiles. It begins in the 720s as a production site but only takes on an urban character in the 760s when it is given a planned layout. In 808, as a result of conflict between Danish and Slavonic interests, Godfred destroyed *Reric* and moved the merchants to Hedeby.

Hedeby, in German *Haithabu*, literally means 'heath settlement'. Its location at the foot of the Jutland peninsula at one end of the fortified rampart, the Danevirke, put it in a commanding position to control east–west trade. The earliest activity in Hedeby dates from the 8th century, when the first jetties were built and a number of workshops were in use. During the 9th century streets were laid out at right angles and parallel to a stream, defining fenced building

6. Aerial view, Hedeby. The curving rampart can clearly be seen; the dense patch of woodland at the north end is the site of the hillfort which overlooked the town.

plots of regular size. Like Birka, the area was enclosed by a semi-circular rampart and protected by a small fort. The harbour was protected by a semi-circular arrangement of piles. There were between 2,000 and 5,000 graves within the rampart, and more outside. The majority of the burials were males, and although most are poor, there are some richly furnished 10th-century chamber graves. It has been suggested that by the 10th century there was a community of between 400 and 1,000 living in Hedeby, their livelihoods based directly or indirectly on trade. Imported materials supported a range of craft industries, including iron working with Swedish ore, the dressing of lava querns from the Mayen area, bronze jewellery production, antler, bone, leather and wood-working, and the manufacture of glass and amber beads. From the early 9th century Hedeby also minted its own coins.

The first Norwegian town has been examined at Kaupang, on the west side of the Oslo fjord. The name literally means 'marketplace', and Kaupang has been identified as Ohthere's *Sciringesheal*. Recent excavations by Dagfynn Skyre have revealed that the laying out of individual plots was preceded by a very short-lived phase of itinerant craft production. Permanent buildings, in use all year round, were then constructed on each of the plots, probably in the early 9th century, but the town was abandoned by the 10th century, possibly reverting to a seasonal market. Kaupang had wide-ranging trading connections. The traded goods include German wine in Rhenish pottery, with glass drinking horns, Danish or Slavonic honey, and Norwegian whetstones. The inhabitants of Kaupang were also melting down silver and the finds include gold and silver which may have arrived as the result of raiding activity, including a Frankish book mount and an Irish brooch.

In the immediate hinterland of Kaupang there is a large farm at Huseby-Tjølling with a bow-sided hall, with imported cornelian beads and glass drinking vessels. Was this the hall of the prefect responsible for controlling the town? There are also a number of distinct cemeteries, including a large cremation cemetery, and a smaller group of high-status boat burials. It has been suggested that, while the cremation graves reflect the local burial rite, the boat burials may be of Danish merchants. Tree ring dating of the jetty at Kaupang proves it was erected sometime after 803 and it is argued that, like Hedeby, Kaupang may have been founded by the Danish King Godfred in the early 9th century in order to control the opposite end of his kingdom.

Finally, Scandinavian urbanism entered a new phase from the latter part of the 10th century, exhibiting more complex organization and the influence of the church. Århus was founded c.900 and was referred to as a bishopric at several points in the 10th century. It may have been established quite quickly, on a 4-hectare site enclosed by the sea and a semi-circular rampart, leading to the suggestion that it was also founded by royal intervention as a military stronghold which nurtured civilian activities.

In Sweden, Birka was replaced by Sigtuna at the end of the 10th century, but initially it had few eastern contacts and international trade really only developed again in the 11th century. Settlement was organized in two rows of narrow building plots, on either side of a 700m stretch of road. The first Swedish coins were minted here in *c.*995, but during the later Middle Ages the trading focus shifted further around Lake Mälar, this time to Stockholm. Lund in Sweden, and Bergen and Oslo in Norway each seem to have been founded in the early 11th century.

The most northerly Scandinavian town was at Trondheim, or *Nidaros*. There is archaeological evidence for a royal farm estate and sporadic activity associated with local chieftains in what was to become the centre of the later town for most of the 10th century; but tradition associates town foundation with King Olaf Tryggvason in the late 990s. Certainly more permanent buildings were erected in the late 10th century, and land was regularly parcelled up. The first proper wooden quays were built on the riverside plots in the mid-11th century, and coins were minted from *c.*1050. Trondheim became an important ecclesiastical centre, particularly through pilgrimage to the cult of St Olav; it had seven churches by the end of the 11th century and the archbishopric was founded in 1152–3. A 60m length of one of the medieval thoroughfares was excavated in 1973–85. It was originally a gravel-surfaced track, running parallel to the shore, but was widened by the mid-11th century and surfaced with wooden planking. The areas fronting the street were occupied by large one-or two-roomed structures, maybe rented out to traders and craftsmen as combined workshops and storehouses. In the centre of the plots there were dwelling houses with wall-benches and fireplaces. Other buildings, identified as bathhouses, cookhouses, storerooms, or latrines, occupied the rear of the plots.

Although towns emerged at different times in different parts of Scandinavia, it is difficult to ignore the ubiquitous role of royal authority in providing the circumstances in which they grew. The towns are not particularly Viking, and the cosmopolitan bustle of merchants and craftsmen would have been familiar throughout

Northern Europe. Nonetheless, they facilitated overseas trade and expansionism, and provided the economic basis for the centralization of power and the growth of a mercantile class.

Chapter 6

Across the ocean: seafaring and overseas expansion

Dragon-headed longships, shields down their sides, their red-and-white striped sails catching the wind, have become an important element of the Viking cliché. What is the reality? Alcuin expressed his horror and indignation at the Viking raid on Lindisfarne in 793 and registered his surprise that it was 'possible that such an inroad from the sea could be made'. For 8th- and 9th-century monks the Vikings were pagans from the sea. In an era when travelling by sea was no doubt easier than arduous journeys by land, were their exploits really so exceptional?

The 11th-century Bayeux tapestry provides, in cartoon form, a narrative of the transport of an early medieval army, its horses and provisions by ship, similar to those believed to have carried Viking raiding parties. The Normans were, after all, direct descendants of the Norseman Rollo. The tapestry shows 'clinker', or plank-built, vessels with brightly coloured sails, which could be drawn up upon a shelving beach, and their masts 'un-stepped', or taken down.

The discovery of a boat burial at Gokstad in Norway, in 1880, provided an archaeological reality to support this picture of Norse nautical prowess. It also contributed to the image of Vikings as adventurous explorers and seafarers skilled in building efficient sailing machines. In 1893 a replica of the Gokstad ship sailed from Bergen to Newfoundland in 28 days. When a second Norwegian ship burial was excavated at Oseberg in 1904, the ornately carved keel also demonstrated the artistic vitality of 9th-century Scandinavia. Its discovery fuelled nationalistic fervour and coincided with the last stage of Norway's struggle for independence, finally achieved in 1905. Tree ring dating has confirmed that the Oseberg ship, built *c.*820, is the oldest surviving combined sailing and rowing ship, with space for 30 oarsmen. Earlier vessels were powered by oars alone and although the keel probably evolved in the 7th century, and sails appear on picture stones from the Baltic island of Gotland at around the same time, there is no surviving mast earlier than at Oseberg. The ship was reused as the burial chamber of a Norwegian princess *c.*834 and although it must have been exceptional, even by 9th-century standards, the shortage of other finds, and the prominence of the discoveries from Oseberg in the Ship Museum in Oslo, meant that this royal barge came to stand as the 'type-vessel' for Viking ships.

All that changed in 1957 when the Danish National Museum commenced salvage of five ships from the bottom of the Roskilde fjord. It emerged that the vessels had been scuttled during the 1070s in order to block the fjord entrance at Skuldelev to protect the royal centre at Roskilde. Although stripped of their fittings, and much repaired, the vessels demonstrate that by the 11th century Scandinavian shipping had evolved into specialized forms for different functions, ranging from highly specialized slender longships for warfare, based on a combination of oars and sail; fuller and more solidly built sailing ships for carrying cargo; plus smaller vessels for fishing and ferrying.

Skuldelev 2 was a slender longship, nearly 30m in length. It was designed for speed, and the transport of 60–80 men and booty, and its mast could be unstepped, allowing it to sail upriver and under bridges. However, analysis of the tree rings has proved that this

7. The Oseberg ship; excavation crew in the mound, 21 September 1904

great Viking symbol was not built in Scandinavia at all. In fact it was constructed in the Dublin area *c*.1042–3 and was probably used in the Irish Sea area for at least 20 years before being repaired (again with Irish timber) and taken to Roskilde. Its planking was formed from good quality oak, and it was probably built in the Scandinavian tradition for a local chieftain as a means of taking part in the normal activities of the Norse in Dublin – slave trading and mercenary activity in Ireland, England, and Wales.

Skuldelev 5 was also a longship but was much smaller and more crudely built. It had been constructed in east Denmark *c*.1040 for a crew of 26. The bottom planking was originally made of new oak timbers, but the sides comprised a mixture of oak, ash, and pine and had been patched with planks taken from other ships. The life of this ship had been stretched to its limits, leading to the suggestion that it was a *leidang* ship, provided as a duty by the peasants of a district who were obliged to deliver and man a ship of 26 rowers. Although by itself it does not prove that this documented 12th-century military levy had Viking Age origins, as has been argued, it does reinforce how Scandinavian sailors were just as capable of keeping old crates afloat as later mariners.

Skuldelev 1 was much broader in relation to its length, and represents the development of the ocean-going trader, or *knorr*. It had a cargo hold amidships, capable of holding up to 40–50 tons, and a deck only at bow and stern. The mast was firmly seated and it relied upon its sail for propulsion, and although it could have carried up to 12 crew, it used oars only when becalmed or for manœuvring. It was built of pine in western Norway, c.1040, but had been repaired twice between 1060 and 1070, latterly with oak from Skåne.

The Skuldelev finds have transformed our knowledge of Scandinavian ships, but the story does not end there. During the construction of the new Roskilde Museum extension to house the Skuldelev finds, a further nine ships from the late Viking Age and Early Middle Ages were discovered. One of them was the largest warship so far found. Roskilde 6, discovered in 1997, was c.36m long. It had been built sometime after 1025, probably in Denmark. The rig consisted of a single square sail, maybe nearly 200 square metres, and it may have had up to 78 rowing stations. It was built of the finest timber with excellent craftsmanship, and was a product of wealth and power found only among the highest ranking members of society.

A similar vessel was also recovered from the harbour at Hedeby. Hedeby 1 has been interpreted as a royal vessel built locally for a crew of 60. It displays exquisite quality; the oak planks are over 10m long; the rivets are exceptionally close. Its construction would have required skilled shipwrights with access to exceptionally large trees and abundant supplies of iron. The vessel was probably only between 5 and 25 years old when it sank, having been used as a fireship, perhaps burnt out during an attack on the harbour *c*.1000. By contrast, Hedeby 2 was possibly a Slavic or Saxon vessel, built *c*.975 as a low-status working boat. It had been constructed partly from reused elements; even the frames had been taken from another boat and consequently did not fit, requiring the support of small additional blocks of wood.

In summary, archaeological discoveries of boats and parts of boats over the last 50 years have helped confirm our image of Vikings as accomplished seafarers, but they also reveal a much more complex picture. There was not just a range of types of vessel, but also a range of investment, from bodged repairs to ornate status symbols fit for the burial of a princess. Research has shown a gradual evolution from Saxon and Frisian rowing boats to the development of specialist classes of ship, amongst peoples whose livelihoods would have depended upon the sea. However, it has also shown that ships were built in what is thought of as a Scandinavian tradition throughout the Irish and North Sea regions. The Skuldelev 2 longship was built in Ireland; in the Dutch harbour of Tiel a 'Viking' ship built of English oak was burnt out and built into the harbour revetments in the early 11th century.

For many of those living in early medieval Europe knowledge of the sea would have been important, and for parts of Scandinavia it was the only way of getting around and so was essential. Norway took its very name from the navigation route, the Norvegur, along its western coast, while the nautical term starboard is derived from the right-hand side of the ship upon which a side rudder, or 'steerboard', was mounted. Over 850 pre-modern boathouses have been recognized in Norway; 250 are concentrated in south-west Norway; there is a second group of 500 in the North. Although not dated precisely to the Viking Age, approximately 250–300 are very large, and although they are too big for a fishing vessel they could have accommodated a longship. There is some evidence that they were used for feasting too and it has been argued that their distribution suggests a military context, linked to early chiefdoms, and later developing into the military levy or *leidang* system.

Without sophisticated navigation instruments sea travel would have relied upon observations of currents, landmarks, and the stars. It has been demonstrated that use of a simple bearing dial would have allowed Viking Age sailors to travel due east or west along a line of latitude, although the method requires the sun to be visible for most of the journey, possibly a big assumption for the North Atlantic. The ability to determine one's longitude, however, only came much later, in the 18th century, with the measurement of speed and time elapsed since departure. Nonetheless, a bearing dial would allow a Norwegian ship to depart from Bergen and sail due west to Shetland, or to sail up the coast before turning west to Iceland, for example. Half of a round disc of wood marked with equidistant notches discovered in 1948 at Narsarsuaq, Greenland, has been taken as proof of the existence of such nautical aids, but sceptics have pointed to the fact that it was found in the remains of what is thought to have been a Benedictine convent and have suggested, rather prosaically, that it was a medieval confessional disc.

So what of the cliché? Viking sails have not survived but we have striped designs from Bayeux. On the Gokstad and Skuldelev 5 ships there are battens for shields to be hung along the sides of vessels. Dragon-prowed ships exist as graffiti and as literary metaphors, but the best we can do archaeologically is a beast-headed bedpost from Oseberg! Dragon ships may only exist as part of the modern Viking stereotype, but the existence of a skilled seafaring people is not in doubt. Both ships and navigational skills enabled the migration of people from Scandinavia from the late 9th to the 11th centuries.

Expansion overseas

Historians have struggled to find a single cause for Viking expansionism, and it is likely that motives changed and evolved through time. Competition for scarce resources against a background of population growth was the underlying factor, but competition may have begun as a search for portable wealth, and developed into the quest for new land.

It has been debated whether Vikings were primarily raiders or traders, but the distinction may not have been a meaningful one. The centralization of power in Iron Age Scandinavia was based upon a gift exchange economy in which chieftains had privileged access to imported goods. Status was based upon portable wealth that could be passed down the social hierarchy as rewards to followers. In the early Viking Age it was the shortage of portable wealth in Scandinavia that was the driving force for overseas expeditions. Scandinavian leaders took tribute from those who were in a weaker position, and in turn passed on gifts in order to acquire status and gain support. If gifts were not forthcoming then they could be extracted by force instead. In the later saga literature strong leaders were characterized as ring-givers since they gave silver arm rings to their followers to secure and reward their allegiance. Silver hoards are characteristic finds in the homelands, and in areas of Viking raids.

When the Hiberno-Norse Vikings were expelled from Dublin c.900 (p. 78) they took with them the 'pay chest' of their army, but in 905 they were forced to bury it in a lead-lined chest on the banks of the River Ribble at Cuerdale, and were never able to recover it. The Cuerdale hoard had been collected over several decades by an international force. It comprised c.7,500 coins, including c.5,000 contemporary Viking issues, c.1,000 Anglo-Saxon coins, and c.1,000 Frankish and Italian coins. There were also c.1,000 pieces of bullion silver in ingots and ornaments, including some complete Irish silver arm rings. In total there was c.40 kg of silver; estimates of its value in today's prices range from £300,000 to £4,000,000.

The Cuerdale hoard was probably amassed through a mixture of trading and raiding activity; slaves acquired through raiding in

Ireland might have been sold in York, for example. Scandinavians played a decisive role in trade in many of the areas where they took political control. They traded not only in luxury goods, but also increasingly in ordinary bulk commodities. They also acted as middlemen between the East and the West, and after Muslim incursions in the Mediterranean closed the traditional trade routes, they opened new ones through the Baltic and Russia. Economic expansion was fuelled by population increase, manufacturing growth, and new wealth – which was itself often derived from plunder and tribute. It was facilitated by Scandinavian political domination, with the fact that exchange was easy within an area under the same language and culture.

Scandinavian lords such as Ohthere operated in several different economic spheres. They took tribute and gifts at home, where social obligation was as important as monetary value. Hoards were part of the process of amassing wealth to be used in gift exchange. Traders regularly exchanged to gain luxury items (particularly silver), to win friends, influence the powerful, and purchase allies. However, when they came to trade their goods and slaves in the blossoming markets of Northern Europe they would meet other merchants with whom they had never previously met and whom they might never meet again. Here it was necessary for royal authority rather than social obligation to ensure fair play, and economic transactions were separated from social relations. The minting of coinage under royal control became necessary to facilitate the conduct of purely monetary transactions.

As gift exchange declined in importance, the ownership of land became more important than portable wealth. Hoarding ended not because peace finally reigned but because the basis of political power changed. Land and estates became the main source of power, not territories and followers, and the later Viking raids were directed to the acquisition of new places to settle. In the North Atlantic there were underpopulated and virgin territories, but in the British Isles land had to be seized from those already inhabiting it, and there were various strategies to accommodate the indigenous population, dependent upon the local balance of power. Viking leaders were often simply able to seize land, from kings and abbeys whose power base they had destroyed, and redistribute it to their followers, although in England there is also documentary evidence for their involvement in cash transactions for the purchase of land. Silver was now used in buying and selling; not in competitive gift-giving.

Vikings in Western Europe

The first recorded raids on Western Europe date from the close of the 8th century. Whether in continental Europe or the North or Irish Seas, raiding followed a similar pattern. Unprotected coastal and riverine sites, including monasteries and markets, were the first targets, normally for small bands of Vikings in two or three ships who returned home as the winter storms began. In the 790s they attacked the Northumbrian monasteries and in 799 raided the Carolingian Empire. The first Viking raid on the Irish coast took place in 795, and movement inland is first recorded *c*.830. From the 830s larger forces raided along the Frisian coast (the modern Netherlands) and devastated the south coast of England. The wealthy trading town of Dorestad was plundered for four successive years in 834–8.

The Viking armies were quick to exploit local rivalries and weakness. After the death of Louis the Pious in 840 the Carolingian Empire was divided amongst his sons. With civil war and independent warlords intent upon carving out their own territory, Viking commanders hastened further fragmentation. In 841 Vikings ravaged Rouen and in 845 an attack on Paris was only prevented by the payment of 7,000 pounds of silver. In 852 a Viking fleet wintered on the Seine and in 853 on the Loire. The fleet continued to exploit these river systems until Charles the Bald built fortified bridges and protected the towns and abbeys, forcing the Viking armies to focus their attention on England.

In 850 a Viking force over-wintered in England for the first time, signalling the beginning of a new phase of more sustained attack by highly mobile forces. In 865 reference is made for the first time to the payment of Danegeld, in return for which the people would be left in peace. The clearest evidence for this phase of Viking activity in Europe comes from Scandinavia itself, where there are thousands of Carolingian and Anglo-Saxon coins.

This extraction of wealth must also have helped weaken the Carolingian Empire, but the Scandinavian impact has otherwise left little trace in the archaeological record in Frankia. There are Scandinavian influenced place names along the line of the Lower Seine to Rouen, but almost all the artefacts are confined to Normandy and Brittany in the north-west. In Normandy, as in England, interaction between the native Franks and Scandinavians led to the rapid formation of a distinctive local Norman culture. There are also a handful of coastal burial sites, including a 10th-century ship burial on the Île de Groix in Brittany. A longship with a smaller boat inside had been dragged along a processional way of standing stones, and then filled with a rich assemblage of objects, including weapons, riding gear, gold and silver jewellery, ivory gaming pieces, smith's tools, and farming equipment. The bodies of an adult male and an adolescent – possibly a sacrifice – were placed in the ship, which was surrounded by 24 shields and set alight. This is the only known example of the burning of a ship as part of the burial rite, although it has become an essential part of the Viking stereotype. In fact it was carried out at a time when most Scandinavian warriors had been converted, and represents the reinvention of a pre-Christian identity in the face of widespread assimilation.

There are other examples of the retention and reinvention of Viking identity in the Scandinavian colonies in the British Isles and the North Atlantic and these form the subject of subsequent chapters. First, however, it is necessary to consider Scandinavian expansion eastwards.

Expansion in the East

While Scandinavians from Denmark and Norway looked predominately westwards, those from Sweden looked eastwards, where they encountered very different cultures. The significance of a Viking presence to the development of Russia has been much debated and views have swung in time with the pendulum of internal Russian politics and the East–West relationship. It has been claimed, alternately, that Scandinavians were responsible for founding the great towns of European Russia (the so-called Normanist view), or that the Russian state was established by people of Slavonic origin (the anti-Normanist view), according to whether the dominant views of the time are pro- or anti-Western. Much depends upon the identity of a people known as the Rus who were invited to bring order to Central Russia in 860–2, and whether they were Slavic or Scandinavian.

There is no dispute that Scandinavians from the Baltic were active down the great Russian river routes such as the Don, the Dnieper, and the Volga. With overland portage to transfer boats and goods from one river to the next they could have reached the Caspian and Black Seas and gained access to the treasures of Byzantium, but did they come as traders or raiders? Over one hundred Swedish rune stones testify to men who died in the East, including many on an ill-fated expedition led by one Ingvar, but the purpose of their journeys is rarely given. Exotic Eastern objects and Byzantine silks are found throughout Scandinavia, and there are over 60,000 Arabic coins, but were these acquired as loot, protection money, tribute, or through trade?

In truth there was probably an element of all four. Tenth-century Arabic texts refer to people described as the Rus as traders in furs and slaves in the Bulghar region. The traveller Ibn Fadlan observed their alien dress styles and their strange mortuary practices, which included the sacrifice of slave girls. He also says that the king of the Rus had a personal retinue of 400 warriors.

The Eastern Emperor in Byzantium (modern Constantinople) had a Varangian bodyguard comprising Scandinavian mercenaries. In 860 there was a famous Viking raid on Byzantium, and in 910–12 a fleet of 16 ships was based in the Caspian Sea, attacking Abaskun, and killing many of the Muslim inhabitants.

How far does archaeological evidence help us understand the nature and extent of activity? The best evidence that peoples of Scandinavian origin lived in Russia is provided by their burials. Up to 26 boat graves are known, including ten from Plakun, near the early trading site at Staraja Ladoga. The burials included people of high social standing, and the presence of women suggests that they were a settled group. At Gnezdovo, near Smolensk, some 600 burials have been excavated out of a large cemetery of *c*.3,000 mounds. These show a variety of burial customs, comprising 80 per cent cremation and 20 per cent inhumation, some in chamber graves. There were also 11 boat graves, although some contained cremations, unknown in Scandinavia. Over a tenth of the burials contain weaponry, but almost as many contain weighing scales and Arabic coins. The richest burials are the chamber graves and although they often contain Scandinavian jewellery, cauldrons, swords, and drinking horns, they also have Byzantine imports. In fact it appears as if the cemetery population at Gnezdovo comprised at least three components: Scandinavians mainly of the 10th century; Slavs in unfurnished cremations, or buried with just a few objects such knives, pottery, single beads, but including females with eastern Slavonic wire rings; and lastly Balts with Moravian-style jewellery.

At Tjernigov, also near Smolensk, there are further chamber graves, many containing double male and female burials, although it has been noted that while the men had Scandinavian weapons and belt fittings, the women never had Scandinavian brooches. Elsewhere, but particularly in those cemeteries associated with important centres are further graves with Scandinavian objects, or goods

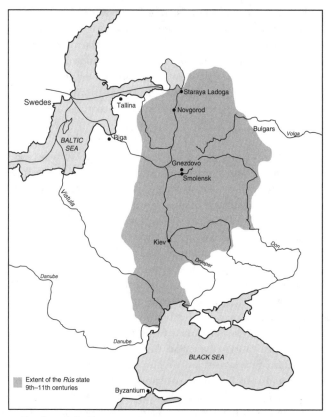

Swedes

Staraya Ladoga

Tallina

Novgorod

BALTIC
SEA

Bulgars

Volga

Riga

Gnezdovo

Smolensk

Vistula

Kiev

Don

Dnieper

Danube

Danube

BLACK SEA

Extent of the *Rús* state
9th–11th centuries

Byzantium

8. Russia and the East

produced locally in a Scandinavian style. Generally these do not
stand out as being particularly rich, nor isolated from other burials
exhibiting Finnish, Baltic, and Slavic customs. Scandinavians,
therefore, appear to have formed one relatively small element in a
very mixed population, and seem to have been regarded as settled
members of the community. Some were mercenary warriors, others
were traders, and it is not always possible to distinguish between
them.

Archaeological research has also revealed considerable consistency in settlement patterns in Russia 900–1200. The cultural landscape of the medieval Rus consisted of clusters of settlements located near rivers and lakes, surrounded by extensive woodlands. Patches of man-made landscape were small compared with the area of unsettled territories, although there was rapid growth in rural settlements from between the late 9th to 11th centuries and the 13th century.

The first towns lay on or near the river routes. Staraja Ladoga was sited where the Scandinavian route into the East splits into two: the Volga and the Dnieper. It was situated not on open water where it would have been exposed to surprise attack, but 12 kilometres up the River Volkhov. The site is on a high bank by a ravine; an earth rampart, enclosing an area of *c.*650,000 square metres, gives further protection. The earliest levels, tree ring dated to 760–840, were built on undisturbed natural soil. Large timber houses were constructed, and some appear to have served as workshops for craftsmen working with glass, bronze, and antler. The buildings are not Scandinavian, however, but built of logs with notched and overlapping ends in a block-house type, familiar from earlier Finnish inhabitants of the region. Furthermore, most of the material from the earliest levels is also native, with some Slavonic imports and a few Scandinavian objects, including an early type of oval brooch. Combs were made here, apparently by itinerant craftsmen who also worked in the Baltic. The settlement was destroyed by fire *c.*860, but was soon rebuilt and fortified with a stone wall before the end of the century. The number of Scandinavian finds increases from this point, and includes a Norse rune stick. The Scandinavian-style boat burials nearby at Plakum also date to this period.

At Ryurik Gorodishche a hillfort site functioned as an administrative, trading and craft-production centre of the 9th century, and may have been a tribute collection centre for a Scandinavian chieftain. It was probably succeeded by Novgorod, known to Scandinavians as Holmgardr. According to the Nestorian Chronicle the first Scandinavians settled there under Rurik in 862, although it had previously been occupied by Slavs. Excavations have revealed a winding timber main street, resurfaced with new planks until *c.*1600. There is not much explicitly Scandinavian material, however, apart from a few items of jewellery.

At Gnezdovo, a 4-hectare unfortified settlement of the 9th century was given sand ramparts and wooden walls *c.*900–25. By 1000 the hillfort contained a cemetery and an irregular settlement and manufacturing site. Craft activities included the working of ferrous and non-ferrous metals, and the manufacture of jewellery, including moulds for casting Scandinavian-style brooches. Iron knives were produced according to a three-fold welding technique which was unknown to the Slavs, and which disappeared with the decline of Gnezdovo, and its replacement by Smolensk. Unlike early Scandinavian trading sites, Gnezdovo was unplanned and appears to have lacked a hinterland; it did not become a town.

Kiev, on the other hand, became the centre of the medieval Russian state. The town was founded in 882 on the west bank of the Dnieper, at a point where the river narrows. The Emperor Constantine recorded that Scandinavians gathered there in early summer, leaving for the journey to Byzantium in June. The town is said to have been ruled by Scandinavian princes, although archaeological evidence suggests that the majority of the population was again mainly Slavonic.

In summary, the post-Glasnost view is that a balance between internal (mainly Slavonic) growth and external Western (Scandinavian) stimulus underpinned the development of medieval Russia. There was already economic and social development amongst the Slavs before the Swedes arrived. The Vikings stimulated and expanded trade, but were not alone in their activities. As in many other areas, they are said to have adopted many native customs and became part of a vigorous mixed group involved in a combination of exchange and raiding which has been labelled 'aggressive trading', although it is not always clear whether this compromise term refers to haggling in the bazaar or to extortion at sword point.

Chapter 7
Settlers in England

For the present-day inhabitants of England, it is the Anglo-Saxons who have generally been regarded as the ancestral English, whereas the Vikings are definitely *them*, not *us*. The English may have a sneaking admiration for their amoral and carefree existence, but apart from a few hotheads who claim they carry Viking blood, they are not really our ancestors. The English language, English laws, customs, and system of government, even the English countryside and villages, are somehow Anglo-Saxon and not North European or Scandinavian, despite the irony that the Angles and Saxons arrived from much the same area as the Danes, some 400 years earlier. It is still Ælfred who was the first king of England, and it was he who united the warring Anglo-Saxon kingdoms against the Viking invader. In 793 there were four Anglo-Saxon kingdoms: East Anglia, Mercia, Wessex, and Northumbria; by 900 there was just one: Wessex.

However, it was Ælfred's own scribes who recorded events in the Anglo-Saxon Chronicle, and since the Vikings did not write history it is little wonder that we have been sold a one-sided story. Historians are now less inclined to accept Wessex propaganda at face value. Although the scale of Scandinavian settlement is still debated, its positive impact is widely acknowledged. Archaeologists have emphasized the Scandinavian contribution to urbanism, to the development of industry, and to the changes taking place in rural settlement patterns; and from new artefact types and artistic styles they are able to talk about a hybrid Anglo-Scandinavian culture. Present-day school children are taught to appreciate ethnic diversity, and in history lessons they learn about multiple waves of raiders and settlers, each contributing to the national character. With England and Denmark once again joined together in a political union for the first time since Cnut, the Vikings have a more positive image.

Academics discussing the scale of Scandinavian settlement in England have danced to the rhythms of the ongoing debate between those who see the history of England as one of successive waves of invaders, and those who emphasize internal evolution and change. According to whom you believe, immigration was confined to a small group of elite land-takers, or it was a secondary mass migration in the wake of the raiding parties. Part of the problem is that the different categories of evidence do not describe a coherent story, and so each discipline has taken a different perspective. The Anglo-Saxon Chronicle records three partitions of land between the Danes and the English in the 870s – in Northumbria, Mercia, and East Anglia. Following the Treaty of Wedmore in 886 a boundary was established between Ælfred and the Danes, running: 'Up the Thames, and then up the Lea, and along the Lea to its source, then in a straight line to Bedford, then up the Ouse to Watling Street'. The area to the north and east of this line later became known as the Danelaw, to distinguish that part of the country where Danish custom prevailed.

Place-name scholars have found that there is some correspondence between their maps of Scandinavian-influenced names and the boundaries of the Danelaw. In Yorkshire, for example, there are 210 place names that end in -by (the Old Norse name for village); in Lincolnshire there are 220, the majority combined with Old Norse personal names. However, it is important to emphasize that the distribution maps show the influence of the Scandinavian language, not the location of Scandinavian settlements. Initially, at least, there

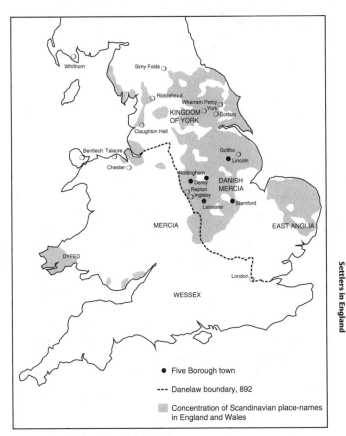

9. Scandinavian activity in England

must have been two distinct Old English and Old Norse language-using communities in the Danelaw, although the languages were so similar that there would have been sufficient mutual intelligibility for most transactions, without the need for widespread bilingualism or for specialist interpreters. During the 10th and 11th centuries, however, there was extensive hybridization and language borrowing between the two cultures. The place-name evidence is late, most names being first recorded in the Domesday Book of 1086, by which time the Anglo-Saxons had been undergoing 200 years of cultural mixing with speakers of Old Norse.

Archaeologically, Scandinavian settlements have been difficult to detect. In the upland areas of northern England, isolated farmsteads such as that at Ribblehead have often been assumed to be the homes of colonists, and further south, the appearance of bow-sided halls at sites like Goltho might indicate the residences of new Scandinavian lords – although of course there is nothing ethnically Scandinavian about the shape or form of a building. At Wharram Percy, Borre-style belt fittings, probably manufactured in Norway, have been found on the site of what became one of the medieval manors, and it seems likely that the village was first laid out with regularly divided plots in the 10th century. This process of village nucleation is repeated throughout lowland England during the 10th century, and may represent part of an ongoing process of land privatization. Former great estates, previously owned by the king or the church, were divided up into smaller units held by individual lords. This process was happening both in the Danelaw and in Wessex and was not a direct result of Viking raids, although the disruption of the monasteries and the subsequent dislocation of landholdings clearly accelerated the process.

The recording of finds recovered by metal-detectorists has also transformed knowledge of settlement patterns. The population of Viking Age England acquired a taste for costume jewellery mass-produced in copper alloy. Although some retain Anglo-Saxon forms, such as the disc brooch, they are frequently decorated with Scandinavian-style motifs, and therefore represent a hybrid culture which it is appropriate to call Anglo-Scandinavian. There are also completely new types, such as tiny copper alloy bells, which may have been amulets or costume fittings. Although they are not known from Scandinavia itself, they have been found in settlements as far apart as Iceland, Scotland, and Yorkshire, and may represent the spread of a fashion developed in the Irish Sea region. Metal objects produced according to Anglo-Scandinavian taste have been found in large numbers in eastern England. Whereas we cannot choose our genes and we can only modify our language to a limited extent, we can choose our jewellery, and these finds indicate widespread acceptance of an Anglo-Scandinavian cultural identity in 10th-century England.

At Cottam, in East Yorkshire, I excavated a settlement first discovered by metal-detectorists. In the 8th and 9th centuries there had been an Anglo-Saxon farmstead, possibly an outlying dependency of a royal estate at Driffield. The residents had been part of a trading network and there were large numbers of low-denomination Northumbrian copper alloy coins, or *stycas*. In the late 9th or early 10th century the Anglo-Saxon farm was abandoned and replaced by a new planned farm set within rectangular paddocks and with a rather grand gated entrance. The new occupants, who from their dress may well have been Scandinavian colonists, were no longer able to buy and sell with coins as the Northumbrian mints had ceased production, but this did not prevent them trading west with York and south of the Humber to Lincolnshire, weighing out bullion to conduct their transactions. They lived in their new farm for only a couple of generations before relocating to the site of what became the planned medieval village.

The Scandinavian settlement also brought major changes to towns and provided a stimulus for the largest urban regeneration since Britain under the Romans. In Mercia and Wessex, systems of fortified towns, or *burhs*, were established by royal decrees in response to the Viking threat. They also functioned as civil and ecclesiastical administrative centres, and mints were established in them. In some cases, such as Chester, Gloucester, Exeter, and Winchester, Roman sites were refortified; in other cases they used natural defences. Elsewhere, such as at Cricklade, Wallingford, and Oxford, new defences were constructed based upon Roman models.

Many became important markets; at Chester a community of Hiberno-Norse traders settled between the Roman fort and the River Dee.

Although Viking raids initially disrupted trade organized through the urban markets or *wics*, at places such as Hamwic (Southampton), Lundenwic (London), and Eoforwic (York), these towns flourished in the 10th century. In most cases the trading sites were brought within, or adjacent to, the walls of the old Roman forts, and were then subject to rapid development. York is the best known, with the street at Coppergate established in the early 10th century, and four tenements used by a variety of merchants, manufacturers, and craftsmen. Within 50 years the pressure on urban space – in common with many other English towns – led to the development of planked two-storey buildings, with cellars for storing raw materials and finished products, and upstairs for living, working, and trading. The city was an important commercial and manufacturing centre and by 900 York's new Viking rulers were minting their own coins. These were partly for propaganda purposes, demonstrating that the Viking kingdom was as respectable as other Western Christian states, but the volume of coinage indicates high levels of transactions. By 1000 York may have had a population of 15,000, dependent upon food supplied from the hinterland, and with access to cereal crops, animals, and marine resources. The Life of St Oswald records that the city was 'enriched with the treasures of merchants, who come from all parts, but above all from the Danish people'.

In the East Midlands the Danes themselves established a series of urban strongholds, described as the Five Boroughs, comprising Derby, Leicester, Lincoln, Nottingham, and Stamford. Excavations have failed to reveal anything specifically Scandinavian about these towns and they may have been based upon English models. Some of the new industries which grew up within their shadow, such as the production of glazed Stamford-ware pottery, may have resulted from immigrants moving in with the Scandinavian traders, but

10. **Excavations in progress at Coppergate, York**

throughout England rural 'cottage' industry was being replaced by
town-based industrialized mass production in response to the new
urban markets.

Erik Bloodaxe (d. 954)

Erik Bloodaxe, Viking leader and King of Northumbria, was the son of Haraldr Finehair, King of Vestfold (872?–*c*.930). Few facts about his life are reliably attested, other than that he was expelled from York in 954, and may have been killed on the Roman road to Cumbria at Stainmore (the modern A66). His fame is due to his prominence in the saga literature, unique for a 10th-century Scandinavian king in the British Isles. Erik is said to have begun his Viking career at the age of 12, meeting his wife Gunnhild on an expedition to the White Sea. Erik became king of Norway on the death of his father, killing several of his brothers and rivals, before being ousted by his younger brother Hákon. Erik next made his way to Orkney, and then to Northumbria, eventually residing in York until his expulsion. Erik also appears in *Egils Saga*, as the enemy of the psychopath and poet Egil Skallagrímsson. Despite pardoning Egil's life in return for a praise poem, Erik was generally given a bad press, with a remarkable career of plunder and homicide. He embodies the modern perception of the Viking world.

Nonetheless, although Viking Age England was thriving, the Vikings themselves have been hard to find. The relative scarcity of identifiable burials of a Scandinavian character in England must lead to the conclusion that – unlike those on the Atlantic margins – most settlers were not buried in their traditional dress. The exceptions are mostly clustered in the North-West and Cumbria, areas where a Scandinavian identity seems to have been maintained for longer, and where most settlers lived in scattered farmsteads and were buried on their farms. A number of individual mound burials, frequently containing weaponry, were generally excavated in the

19th century, at sites such as Aspatria, Hesket in the Forest, and Claughton Hall. They follow similar burial practices to those observed on the Isle of Man (p. 85). The only cemetery was discovered in 2004 by a metal-detectorist, on a low hill overlooking the village of Cumwhitton, near Carlisle. It comprised just six burials – four males and two females – buried with weaponry and jewellery. A mound had been raised over one of the males.

In lowland and eastern England such burials are extremely scarce and it appears that Scandinavian cultural identity was rarely reflected in the burial rite. Newcomers in these areas may have often joined established settlements and may have been accommodated within existing Anglo-Saxon graveyards. Another recent discovery, at Adwick-le-Street, near Doncaster, provides a clear exception. A woman had been buried with a non-matching pair of oval brooches, of late 9th-century date, and fragments of an iron knife and key or latch-lifter. A small copper-alloy bowl, probably manufactured in the Celtic West, had been placed at her feet. Isotope analysis of her teeth shows she originated from the Trondheim area of Norway, or possibly north-east Scotland. There is no evidence for settlement or other burials in the locality and she must represent an isolated death.

The other exceptions are provided by two remarkable cemeteries which have been associated with the over-wintering of the Great Army at Repton, in 873–4. Having taken over the Mercian royal shrine at Repton, the Viking army constructed a massive D-shaped encampment, using the River Trent to protect the flat side of the D, and the tower of the Anglo-Saxon church as a gatehouse. In Anglo-Saxon England power could be acquired through association with sanctity and several accompanied burials were placed immediately adjacent to the shrine of the martyred St Wigstan, including the grave of a warrior who had met a particularly grisly death. The man in grave 511 had been killed by a slashing sword blow to his inner thigh, as well as having a sharp object thrust through the socket of an eye; given the damage to the inside of his rib cage there is also a suggestion that he had been disembowelled. He was buried with a sword which had been broken and replaced in its fleece-lined scabbard, a knife and a key. He wore a silver Thor's hammer amulet at his neck, and a jackdaw leg bone and a boar's tuck had been placed between his legs, possibly symbols of Oðinn and Freyr respectively. Outside and to the west of the encampment the Viking army had also desecrated a second mausoleum, levelling a two-roomed structure, and burying an important warrior in the centre of one of the rooms, arranging the reinterred remains of at least 250 individuals around him. A group of four young males, buried adjacent to this mound, may have been sacrificial victims. It has been argued that the charnel deposit, comprising 80 per cent males, may represent warriors of the Viking army, although it has also been suggested that they may have been the Anglo-Saxon monks, either killed in the attack, or disturbed from their graves.

I excavated an alternative candidate for the war cemetery of the Great Army at Heath Wood, on a promontory overlooking Repton and the flood plain of the Trent, 4 kilometres to the south-east. Some 59 mounds can now be identified, in a number of clusters. Some of the mounds were constructed over the cremation pyres of the deceased. The charcoal hearths had been raked over but they include fragments of burnt swords and shields, as well as the cremated bones of sacrificed horses and dogs, and joints of meat. Other mounds appeared to be empty at first but, in one, some small token offerings of a few fragments of burnt bone and a ringed pin were discovered. Perhaps these were cenotaph-style memorials to warriors who had died and been cremated elsewhere, and were represented by small parcels of bone and personal items which had been brought back to Heath Wood. The cremation cemetery at Heath Wood is unique in the British Isles and appears to evoke pre-Christian burial rites in Scandinavia, as if some sections of the campaigning army felt it important to emphasize their Vikingness, while others preferred to be buried adjacent to the Mercian shrine. Whereas Heath Wood was short-lived, the cemetery at Repton continued in use for burials in Scandinavian character into the 10th

Ivarr the Boneless (d. *c*.873)

Ivarr was one of the leaders of the Viking Great Army that invaded England in 865 and is said to have been the son of Ragnar Lodbrok ('Leather Breeches'), who led the sack of Paris in 845. In the later saga literature he is described as lacking bones, the result of a curse placed on Ragnar by his second wife, who warned him not to consummate their marriage until three nights had passed. Ragnar refused to wait, and as a result Ivarr was born. Some have argued that 'boneless' is a mistranslation of 'childless' but the sagas recount how Ivarr was unable to walk and had to be carried on a shield. It has been suggested that he suffered from brittle bone disease.

When Ivarr defeated the Northumbrians at York in 867 their leader Osbert was killed in the battle, and his rival Ælla was put to death by a form of ritual murder known as the 'blood-eagle'. One graphic description says that 'They caused the bloody eagle to be carved on the back of Ælla, and they cut away all of the ribs from the spine, and then they ripped out his lungs', although this account has often been dismissed as later folklore or mistranslation.

Ivarr died in Dublin in 873. According to legend his body was brought back to England. Martin Biddle and Birthe Kjølbye-Biddle have suggested that Ivarr was the warrior buried in the centre of the mausoleum at Repton, although many doubt this.

century, including the erection of a hogback tombstone (see below).

It is significant that, while 9th-century graves are rare, in the 10th century subsequent generations of Scandinavian settlers may also have abandoned grave-goods but developed distinctive stone monuments to mark their graves. In northern and eastern England in particular they borrowed the Anglo-Saxon and Irish custom of erecting stone crosses at monastic sites, and turned them into individual memorials for the founder burials of rural graveyards. At Middleton in North Yorkshire, for example, there is a small group of warrior crosses, including one which depicts an armed warrior on the front, and a dragon-like beast on the reverse, and another which shows a hunting scene.

The so-called hogback tombstones reflect another newly invented type of monument. These low grave memorials have arched backs, like bow-sided halls; some are grasped at each end by pairs of beasts, sometimes identified as muzzled bears. Their inspiration may have come from recumbent stone grave slabs of the early Scandinavian rulers of England, such as those found under York Minster, combined with elements of Irish house shrines. Although examples have been found as far afield as northern Scotland and south-western England, the distribution is focused in North Yorkshire, within the territory of the Viking kings of York and Dublin. Both the crosses and the hogback stones date from the first part of the 10th century and may reflect the arrival of later generations of Hiberno-Norse settlers from Ireland, following their expulsion from Dublin, for whom it was important to preserve a Viking identity.

The new Anglo-Scandinavian lords were Christianized, and much of the sculpture incorporates Christian and pre-Christian themes, such as the cross from Gosforth in Cumbria, which shows a Crucifixion scene populated with figures in Scandinavian costume on one side, and a scene from Ragnarok, the end of the world, on

11. Middleton warrior, North Yorkshire

the reverse. They were also responsible for the great boom in church
building in the 10th and 11th centuries. In Anglo-Saxon England
there was a system of minster churches under which small

communities of monks served the large estates. These had collapsed during the Scandinavian settlement and the new landowners now constructed private chapels on their estates, many of which developed into parish churches serving the local community. At Wharram Percy there is 8th- and 9th-century sculpture relating to an earlier, possibly minster church, but a small timber church was established on a new site in the 10th century. This was enlarged in the 11th century into a stone church with a separate nave and chancel. The church became the focus for burials of the early lords of the manor, including some marked by recumbent stone slabs, and many of the early burials around the church have been radiocarbon dated to the 10th century. An Old English inscription on the sundial at the site of the Anglo-Saxon minster at Kirkdale provides a graphic illustration for this process of Anglo-Scandinavian privatization. It relates how Orm, son of Gamal – both Old Norse names – bought the minster when it was tumbled down and ruined, and erected a new church on the site in 1055–65, the decade before the Battle of Stamford Bridge.

In England, therefore, there is evidence for a complex sequence of assimilation between peoples of different language, culture, and religion, and the creation of hybrid identities, over at least 200 years. The following chapters will look at the situation in other parts of the British Isles, where the native societies may not have been so economically or politically advanced.

Chapter 8

Raiders and traders around the Irish Sea

The areas bordering the Irish Sea rarely featured in contemporary written sources but were of strategic importance to Scandinavian raiders and settlers. Cumbria has already been considered and this chapter will focus on the evidence for a Scandinavian presence in Ireland, Wales and the Isle of Man. The Hebrides, which formed the more northerly extent of this cultural zone, will be considered in the next chapter. There is also evidence for Scandinavian activity in south-west Scotland and along the Solway Firth. At Whithorn, a largely undocumented monastic site was destroyed by fire and abandoned in the 830s. It was reoccupied later in the 9th century, by a community with Scandinavian connections. By the 11th century it was a thriving trading post, with square timber houses which parallel examples from Dublin. From the Iron Age these areas had been united by their easy access to the sea, and they shared a hybrid Hiberno-Norse identity, born of interaction between an indigenous Celtic population and an incoming Scandinavian one.

Ireland

By the late 8th century Ireland was a centre for art, literature, and learning. Despite the lack of unified kingship the Irish elite had developed the concept of an Irish identity, based on language, culture, and religion, and defined and justified through genealogy and origin myths. It was in contrast to this that incoming Vikings were seen as *gaill*, or foreigners. The Vikings have continued to be seen as outsiders – the Irish have looked back to their Celtic heritage for their roots, although the Vikings have been credited with the establishment of the major Irish towns. As is the case in England, there is actually considerable evidence for the development of a hybrid culture in Ireland. Although many of the settlers may have shared a common Norwegian ancestry they are unlikely to have arrived direct from Scandinavia, and they also adopted aspects of Celtic culture. It is therefore often appropriate to describe them as Hiberno-Norse.

It is not as if the Vikings were the only ones looting monasteries. Raiding was endemic in early Christian Ireland and there are at least 30 recorded attacks by Irish raiders prior to the first recorded Norwegian raid on Rechru (probably Rathlin Island, County Antrim) in 795. Up to the early 10th century there is always a clear distinction between Norse and Irish; thereafter the differences become blurred. The raids follow a similar pattern to those recorded in England. From the 830s isolated coastal attacks on monastic sites give way to systematic expeditions inland by larger fleets, and the construction of fortified camps, known as *longphorts*.

In 841 a stronghold was established as *Dubh-linn*, the 'black pool', at a crossing point over the River Liffey. Dublin, under Olaf the White, emerged as a small and powerful kingdom, until the Norse were ousted by an Irish coalition in 902, and 'abandoned a good number of their ships, and escaped half-dead after they had been wounded and broken', probably fleeing to north-west England. A short period of relative peace was followed by renewed raiding and in 917 the base at Dublin was re-established; by the mid-10th century it ruled over a substantial hinterland and written sources describe Dublin as the centre of the slave trade. With the Norman conquest of Ireland in the 1160s the Norse towns became the property of the English crown. By the 12th century all Irish structures were attributed to the Norse, because it was believed that the Irish were incapable of building them. The Welsh writer and cleric Giraldus Cambrensis (1146–1223) wrote that 'the Irish attach no importance to castles, they make the woods their strongholds and the bogs their trenches'.

Viking Dublin was rediscovered in the 19th century. At least four separate cemeteries and a number of single graves were found in and around Dublin, totalling *c.*70–80 male burials and about ten female burials. All are assumed to date from the 60-year period between 841 and 902. The largest concentration was discovered in 1841 in railway cuttings near Kilmainham gaol; a second concentration was found 800 metres further west along the ridge, at Islandbridge. In both cases the burials were inserted amongst unaccompanied Christian cist graves. All appear to have been inhumations: there were *c.*40 swords, *c.*20 spears and shields, and a few oval brooches from female costume. Some of the grave-goods, including weights and scales, suggested trading activities; there were also shears, sickles, tongs and pincers, spindle whorls, and needle cases.

As a result of urban redevelopment, subsequent archaeological excavation has also focused upon Dublin, and has concentrated on the investigation of its origins. The town was enclosed by an earthen bank in the 10th century; a second larger bank was built outside this around the 11th-century town. There were extensive excavations from 1961–81 at High Street, Winetavern Street, and Woodquay. The material has been taken as evidence of predominant, or exclusively, Hiberno-Norse occupation from an early period. The post and wattle houses and workshops have no direct parallels and may have been an Irish type, or may have been influenced from England during the 10th-century re-establishment. They had internal roof-bearing posts, wattle and daub walls, with rounded corners, and a door in each gable wall. The interiors had central hearths with narrow wall benches; there were sometimes small cubicles at each end.

At Fishamble Street extensive excavations have revealed a long sequence of occupation, with Anglo-Saxon-style buildings in the late 9th century, replaced by Hiberno-Norse buildings developed within 14 contiguous plots along the street from *c.*920 to the 11th century. No stables or byres have been found and the animal bones show that meat must have been brought from outside the town, although Finbar McCormick has suggested that the high proportion of pig bones suggest that pigs were kept in the backyards of the properties, maybe reflecting uncertainty over the food supply. The proportion of pigs is much lower in York where the Anglo-Scandinavian kingdom had command of a large area, but is similar to that from Hedeby, which may imply a similar insecurity with regards to its hinterland.

In 2004 another *longphort* settlement was discovered by the river at Woodstown, in south-east Ireland. An early medieval ditched enclosure was recut in the 9th century. It contained settlement traces, including timber houses, with much evidence of ships and perhaps ship construction, including large numbers of iron rivets. Over 170 lead weights have been recovered, as well as evidence for metal-working. Weaponry, including a grave outside the enclosure, containing a sword, spear, axe, shield, honestone and ringed pin, also indicates a date around the mid-9th century for the beginning of Hiberno-Norse activity. Occupation terminates *c.*1050, which is when excavation has revealed that 14 urban plots were established alongside Peter Street in Waterford, 2 kilometres away. There may be a similar site at Annagassan in County Louth. An irregular circular area surrounded by a bank and ditch may indicate the site of the *longphort* which annals record was established in 841.

Evidence for activity outside these semi-urban centres is sparse and it appears that there was little Hiberno-Norse settlement within rural Ireland: 80 per cent of known Scandinavian-style burials come from within 5 kilometres of Dublin. Ring forts and crannogs produce Scandinavian-influenced objects, but none can be pointed to as Norse dwellings. The only clear Hiberno-Norse rural site is a coastal haven, occupied from the 10th to early 12th centuries. Beginish Island, off the west coast of County Kerry, is adjacent to the early monastery on Church Island. It was initially excavated in the 1950s and interpreted as an early medieval settlement with some Norse acculturation in a second phase. However, new work has questioned whether there really are two phases and has also confirmed the Hiberno-Norse character to the site, with a runic inscription and other Hiberno-Norse artefacts. The settlement includes eight houses and a number of animal shelters. One of the buildings incorporates a semi-sunken area which has been seen as a fusion of native Irish building traditions and architectural features, such as cellars, transmitted through Scandinavian towns.

Other evidence also suggests that Hiberno-Norse settlement was limited to southern and eastern Ireland, and to the semi-urban centres, but that alliances were formed with local kings who controlled the rural hinterlands. There are many Hiberno-Norse silver hoards in Ireland, comprising 53 coinless hoards of arm rings and ingots, 16 mixed hoards of coins and metalwork, and 41 coin hoards, predominantly made up of Anglo-Saxon and Anglo-Scandinavian coins from East Anglia and Northumbria, but also incorporating Arabic issues. John Sheehan has identified that whereas those hoards which include coins are found in the south and east, the coinless hoards are spread throughout Ireland, in areas not controlled by the Hiberno-Norse, and many come from ring forts, the bases of local chieftains. Few hoards contain fragmented hack-silver ingots and coins, representing ongoing exchange and classic economic activity. The majority of hoards apparently relate to tribute rather than trade. The Hiberno-Norse formed military alliances with local rulers and gift exchange may have been part of this process. The arm rings, in particular, may represent the payment of tribute from Dublin, designed to buy the allegiance of Irish kings.

Wales

The inhabitants of Wales have focused almost exclusively upon their Celtic past, and there has been little interest in Vikings. By the 9th century Wales consisted of a number of independent kingdoms, united in part by Christianity, and this native elite are generally seen as the ancestral Welsh. Old Norse had relatively little impact on Welsh and, apart from along the coast, there are relatively few Scandinavian-influenced place names. The archaeological evidence comprised a few isolated artefacts such as a glass bead from Hen Gastell (Swansea) and a ringed pin from Caerwent (Monmouthshire). There was little evidence for settlement, other than a handful of burials, including a skeleton buried with an iron spearhead in a slab-lined grave, discovered during the excavation of a cesspit for a new house at Talacre (Flintshire) in 1932, and a lone individual discovered in 1945 on the beach at Benllech in Anglesey, along with a number of iron coffin nails and an antler comb. A single hogback is known from Llanddewi Aber-arth (Ceredigion), and the crosses at Penmon (Anglesey) and Maen Achwyfan (Flintshire) show Scandinavian influence.

The accepted picture has therefore been that Vikings had little impact on Wales, apart perhaps from some isolated enclaves. Nonetheless, although written sources are scarce there are a few recorded raids, and it is likely that there was extensive contact and some settlement. The first recorded raid was in 852, when Cyngen of Powys was slain by 'gentiles', probably Vikings. There was also intensive raiding from c.950, following the death of Hywel Dda, king of Gwynedd and Deheubarth, and coinciding with the expulsion of Erik Bloodaxe from York in 954. Viking armies attacked coastal lowlands and religious centres such as Penmon, Caer Gybi (near Holyhead), Tywyn (Gwynedd), and St David's (raided 11 times between 967 and 1091). In 987 south Wales suffered attacks from an army which operated until 1002, when it was paid off with tribute in silver. There are 11 silver hoards from Wales, all from coastal areas. A hoard of five silver arm rings was found at Red Wharf Bay, on Anglesey, in the late 19th century. Recent excavation by Mark Redknap at the nearby site at Llanbedrgoch has provided dramatic evidence for Viking activity.

Red Wharf Bay forms a large natural harbour, but the settlement at Llanbedrgoch was built on a natural routeway from the landing site, about one kilometre from the sea, but adjacent to a freshwater spring. It begins in the 7th–8th centuries as a native settlement comprising a ditched and banked enclosure encircling a number of wooden buildings constructed in the local tradition of mixed circular round houses and rectangular halls. In the 9th century the enclosure boundary was enhanced with a massive dry-stone wall, high and wide enough to carry a wall-walk, indicating the need to upgrade the defences. Inside there were at least six late 9th-/early 10th-century rectangular halls, including three resting upon sill beams, and two with traces of stone flagged floors. Both the form of the buildings and the evidence for wall benches suggests Scandinavian influence. The buildings were linked by a paved road, 3 metres wide, to an oval spring pool, accessed by stone steps.

Although the animal bone assemblage and presence of quern stones suggests the settlement had an agricultural basis, Llanbedrgoch also had wide trading contacts. There were English coins from Canterbury and Northumbria, Carolingian deniers, and a fragment of an Arabic dirham. There were also 19 lead weights and nine fragments of hack silver. Scandinavian influence is also indicated by the discovery of 11 10th-century ringed pins, four small ornamental bronze bells, and a Borre-style belt buckle; a large whetstone with a bronze ferrule in the shape of a helmet indicates warrior status. Iron forging took place on site, and there were 1,300 iron nails, including rivets from ship repair and over 50 knife blades. There was also casting of non-ferrous metals, in copper alloy, silver, and lead, and antler and leather working. Outside the enclosure five bodies had been unceremoniously dumped in the ditch. One had been thrown on top of a child; his wrists had been tied behind him, and he had suffered a sharp blow to the left eye. Another adult had been placed face down with his arms tied in front of him. These must represent the victims of a raid. Llanbedrgoch was an early princely site or estate centre, and became an important focus for trade in the 9th and 10th centuries. It is very tempting to see the bodies as evidence that it was attacked by Vikings, and possibly occupied by them.

The Isle of Man

The Isle of Man first appears as a historic entity, along with the Western Isles, under its first Norwegian king, Godred Crovan (1079–95), and it had a series of Norse rulers until it was ceded by Norway to Alexander III of Scotland in 1266. The Scandinavian overlay on Man was considerable and the present-day Manx are proud of their Viking heritage. The Manx Parliament – the Tynwald – traces its origins to the meetings of the Norse open-air assembly, or Thing, and still assembles annually at Tynwald Hill, St John's, to promulgate those laws passed during the previous year. Many believe that the basic land unit, the *treen*, each with its chapel or *keeil*, is Norse, although others have suggested it may even be pre-Norse. It has also been argued that the number of surviving Scandinavian place names is only compatible with a substantial Norse settlement, and even that Man was for a while completely Norse-speaking, until Gaelic was reintroduced *c*.1300, although others have claimed that the Scandinavian element was confined to the ruling elite and chief landowners.

Archaeologically, it has been hard to find traces of Norse settlements, which may be under modern farms. There are few excavated sites, other than reoccupied coastal promontories such as Cronk ny Merriu and Close ny Chollagh, and upland shielings, such as Doarlish Cashen and the Braaid. Given the likely continuity of Norse building styles these sites are hard to date.

The burial record is more informative, and there is a relatively large number – over 25 – for such a small island. Many are under low mounds overlooking the sea and they appear to indicate competition for land ownership and the importance of using the landscape to lay claim to farms. During the Second World War, the German archaeologist, Gerhard Bersu, was interned on the Isle of Man as an enemy alien and was allowed to excavate a number of sites, including Balladoole. Here a boat grave had been superimposed upon a Christian cemetery, disturbing several recent burials. The ship was a small rowing boat in which a male was the main burial. He was buried with riding equipment and a number of costume items, including a Carolingian silver buckle and a Hiberno-Norse ringed pin. A substantial wooden pole had been erected at the edge of the mound, which was covered by a layer of cremated bones from sacrificial animals.

Bersu also excavated a chamber grave at Ballateare, on the north-west coast. A young male had been placed in a coffin at the foot of the chamber. He was buried with a sword – broken into three pieces and replaced in its scabbard – and wrapped in his cloak. A shield and two spears – also mutilated – had been put into the burial pit. A mound had been thrown up over the burial, in which cremated animal offerings had again been placed – along with the skeleton of a young woman who had been killed by a sword cut which had removed the top of her skull. A large pole had again been erected over the mound.

These burials, and other accompanied graves from the Isle of Man, have been dated to the late 9th or early 10th centuries. They are unlike the majority of Scandinavian graves, but they have come to stand for the Viking stereotypical warrior burial, with young men buried with all they need for Valhalla – their weapons, their horses and hounds, and even their slave girls. It is as if, in the competitive environment facing the first colonists, it was necessary to develop and exaggerate a Viking identity, as the defining part of who they were, and what they stood for.

By contrast, amongst over 300 cist burials in an early cemetery on St Patrick's Isle, Peel, only seven included any form of grave-goods, and most of these were costume items. Only the so-called 'Pagan Lady' stood out, with her necklace, comb, knives, shears, workbag, and cooking spit, or sorceress' staff. However, she was not wearing Scandinavian dress, which has led to the suggestion that she was a native Celt who had married a settler. The Peel cemetery appears to represent an alternative strategy of assimilation, and within a few generations the Hiberno-Manx elite were being buried in churchyards, under stone cross slabs. As in England, there was a flourishing school of stone sculpture when the Norse arrived, and following their conversion they produced a series of distinctive crosses from 930–1020, frequently combining Christian elements with Scandinavian mythology. At Kirk Andreas church, Sigurd is shown in a conical helmet, roasting three slices of dragon heart over flames. The thumb of his other hand is in his mouth, the tasting of the dragon's blood providing a crude metaphor for the Christian Eucharist. A second cross shows Oðinn, with spear and raven, his foot in the jaws of Fenrir, the wolf, counterbalanced on the other face by a Christian scene of a figure holding a book and cross.

Many of the crosses incorporate runic inscriptions. Most are commemorative and follow a common formula of 'N put this cross up in memory of M'. Of the 44 named individuals, 22 have Norse names, while 11 have Celtic ones. Some were erected in the memory of women, including another example from Kirk Andreas, where 'Sandulfr the Black raised this cross for his wife Arinbjörg'. The earliest surviving runes, from the 10th century, show a clear connection with Norway, but at the same time they show Norsemen accommodating to a Western tradition which has Celtic elements, and the development of a new hybrid cultural identity.

As in England, therefore, it is impossible to speak of a pure Viking cultural identity in the Irish Sea region, although we can observe different strategies of accommodation between raiders and settlers, sometimes emphasizing their cultural difference, and often creating new cultural norms. As we travel northwards, in the next chapter, we will visit areas where it has been argued that the Norse achieved complete cultural dominance.

Chapter 9
Vikings and Picts: genocide or assimilation?

Interpretations of the character of Norse settlement in the Northern and Western Isles embrace the full spectrum of possible relationships between the Norse and the native Picts – from wholesale genocide to peaceful assimilation. Modern genetic evidence is consistent with large folk migration to the Northern Isles, and smaller scale settlement in the Western Isles, but both genetics and place names lack chronological resolution. The Hebrides may have been repopulated by Celtic peoples during the Middle Ages and the high proportion of Scandinavian ancestry in Orkney and Shetland may relate to the long period of close political, economic, and social ties with Norway, maybe commencing before the Viking Age. On balance, the archaeological evidence implies large-scale migration, followed by Norse political, linguistic, and cultural domination, but with some coexistence of indigenous and immigrant identities, expressed differently in each area.

The Hebrides

The Hebrides were linked with the Isle of Man as a single kingdom under the Lordship of the Isles, and shared a Norse inheritance, including traces of a ship levy and clinker-built vessels. It has been argued that the linguistic evidence suggests Gaelic was a later overlay on an almost entirely Old Norse-speaking population, although the place names are a mixture of Gaelic and Old Norse.

Much of the archaeological evidence was discovered so long ago that its value is limited. The picture has been dominated by graves, often chance discoveries as a result of erosion of sand dunes, such as Machrins on Colonsay and Ballinby on Islay. We do know the dead were dressed in full Scandinavian costume, and were well equipped. At Kiloran Bay (Colonsay), and Carn a'Bharraich (Oronsay), they were placed in rowing boats. The cemetery of a small community has been excavated more recently at Kneep on the Isle of Lewis. It includes men, women, and children, some buried with grave-goods, and some without. Isotope analysis of the teeth of a middle-aged woman buried in the late 10th century and dressed in traditional Norwegian folk costume reveals that she had been brought up in western Scotland. As a second-generation settler it is significant that, in death, her relatives were still keen to dress her in Scandinavian costume. As on the Isle of Man it appears that the Hebridean Norse settlers were negotiating their cultural identity through an emphasis on Scandinavian dress and custom. Unlike the Isle of Man, it seems that this strategy embraced their wives as well.

Norse settlements have been identified within grass-covered mounds on the sand dunes of the *machair*. Recent excavations on North and South Uist tell a similar story of takeover of native sites, with limited cultural continuity. At the Udal, on North Uist, characteristic Norse longhouses were built amongst the ruins of Pictish farms, on five settlement mounds, although the first structure built by the new occupants was a defensive enclosure, on the highest point of the site. New Norse styles of pottery, metalwork and combs appear, and the introduction of ceramic platters for baking barley cakes indicates a change in cuisine as well.

On South Uist settlement mounds are found throughout the *machair* and indicate that although farms again kept the same location from prehistoric times, new artefacts and new buildings appear during the Norse period. At Cille Phaedir a 10th-century timber hall represents a radical departure from local building tradition, accompanied by the characteristic consumption of barley cakes. At Bornish, a long-lived Pictish settlement was levelled during the creation of a 10th-century Norse farmstead, and the builders appear to have feasted before they laid the floor. By the late 11th century they were living in a classic Scandinavian-style bow-sided hall, 20 metres long, with substantial stone footings, robbed from an adjacent Pictish structure. The inhabitants of Bornish were more affluent – they were importing pottery from Wessex, and making antler combs. They were also maybe displaying mixed cultural messages. Niall Sharples has suggested that a Norwegian bone mount was deliberately buried because of its personal association with the owner, while houses were rebuilt overlapping earlier structures to demonstrate an ancestral link with the past.

Orkney

The Life of Findan, a 9th-century continental source, is the most important contemporary document regarding the settlement of Orkney. It provides an apparently historical account of an Irish aristocrat's escape from Norse slave traders on Orkney and his subsequent stay with a bishop, generally assumed to have been a Pict; the incident is dated c.840. The accepted origin myth, however, is to be found in the *Orkneyinga Saga*, written c.1192–1206. It claims that Orkney was settled by Earl Rognvald, fleeing from Norway in the 9th century, and it paints a vivid picture of life in Norse Orkney. Certainly from the mid-9th to the 12th centuries Orkney was the political focus of a semi-independent Norse state, whose ambit extended into Caithness. It did not become part of Scotland until 1468 when it was given to James III as part of the dowry of Margaret of Denmark.

A few place names and carved Pictish symbol stones and settlements indicate an indigenous pre-Norse Pictish population, but Scandinavian names obliterated all but a handful of the indigenous names. They extend to the smallest farmstead and every landscape feature and suggest little interaction.

Excavation of a number of sites around the Bay of Birsay indicates Norse takeover of an embryonic native power centre on the tidal promontory. According to the *Orkneyinga Saga* Earl Thorfinn 'had his permanent residence at Birsay, where he built and dedicated to Christ a fine minster, the seat of the first Bishop of Orkney'. In the second half of the 9th century, Pictish buildings are overlain by rectangular structures ascribed to the Norse. A number of substantial Norse halls were constructed, with wall benches and box beds. Iron-working took place on the island, and silver was also melted down. The community cannot have been self-sufficient, however, and joints of beef and mutton were brought from farms in the bay, such as that at Buckquoy. Here successive generations of cellular buildings in distinctive Pictish figure-of-eight form were replaced by rectangular halls, although Pictish artefacts continued in use, indicating some continuity in population. At Pool, on Sanday, there is a clearly identifiable period of overlap between the

12. **Brough of Birsay: aerial view**

two cultural groups. Pictish buildings were adopted and reused by inhabitants who had access to Norse material, particularly soapstone.

Altogether *c*.130 Scandinavian-style burials have been recognized on Orkney, a number consistent with significant population migration, and reflecting a more broadly-based settlement than in the Hebrides. All can be placed within 850–950, although most were discovered in the 19th century and records are poor.

The cemetery at Westness on Rousay has been excavated relatively recently. It consisted of 32 inhumations, but only eight graves – four male and four female – were accompanied. One grave was of a mother in her twenties, buried with her baby. She had been dressed wearing a pair of oval Norse brooches and a string of beads, but also wore a remarkable silver and gold penannular Celtic brooch. This wealthy woman may have been the head of the founding family. Two male warriors were each buried in small rowing boats. At least one had died in battle as the broken tips of four arrows were lodged in his back. The rest were buried without grave-goods in stone-lined cists, and these probably represent the graves of the pre-Norse population. Their position was marked on the surface by boulders, and none had been disturbed by the Norse. On the same promontory there was a boat house and a farmstead comprising a large hall furnished with low wall benches either side of the hearth, and two byres: one for cattle, and one for sheep.

Another boat burial was found in 1991, eroding out of a low cliff at Scar, on Sanday. The boat was a small rowing vessel which – from the presence of igneous rock particles in the caulking – must have been built in Norway, and brought to Orkney by a larger vessel. A woman in her seventies had been given pride of place in the centre. Her grave-goods included a maplewood box, an iron cooking spit or weaving batten, and a fine whalebone plaque, of north Norwegian type. She was also accompanied by a child, aged about 10, and a male in his thirties who had been squashed into one end of the boat;

13. Westness, Rousay. Male boat grave with the prow and stern packed with stones to create a central chamber for the body

indeed his foot may have been broken in order to force him into the space. Nonetheless, he was no slave for he carried a comb, a sword, and a quiver of arrows, as well as 22 whalebone gaming pieces. Although the objects would place the burial in the late 9th century, radiocarbon dating suggests a date closer to the mid-10th century, indicating that many of the objects were heirlooms and that this was a group maintaining an old cultural and religious identity in the face of growing Christianization of the Norse colonists.

At St Magnus on Birsay, and at Deerness, there were private stone chapels as early as the 10th century, and by the 11th century considerable resources were invested in church building throughout Orkney. At Newark Bay a rectangular stone building underlay the later church. It was surrounded by c.250 burials which respected it apart from two burials inserted into the floor. Two 10th-century coins were found beneath the stone floor and 20 radiocarbon dates from the burials are consistent with mid-10th-century usage of the cemetery. It has been suggested that the occurrence of *Papa* place names on Orkney reflects the survival of Pictish Christian enclaves that were responsible for the early conversion of the Norse. It seems clear, however, that by 900 the Picts had been eclipsed – politically, linguistically, culturally, and socially. Their aristocracy had been displaced by Norse war leaders and only at the lower levels of society can survival of a native element in the population be perceived.

Shetland

Shetland appears fleetingly in the *Orkneyinga Saga*, but it is generally assumed that it was colonized at the same time as Orkney, and enjoyed close connections with Norway. Hitherto there has been little archaeological investigation of Norse sites, and our knowledge has relied upon Jarlshof where, in 1934, Alexander Curle excavated the first Norse farmstead to be identified in the British Isles. Although it was described as a township, Jarlshof was never more than a farmstead, rebuilt many times, with the Norse longhouses erected adjacent to a Pictish broch. At Old Scatness Norse artefacts have also been found within an abandoned broch, suggesting that here and at Jarlshof they may have been targeting Pictish estate centres. The Norse finds coincide with economic changes, including the introduction of flax cultivation (possibly for linen for use in fishing nets) and more intensive exploitation of marine resources, although barley and oats were still grown.

Fieldwork by Stefan Stumann Hansen on the small island of Unst has sought to map fragments of a Norse landscape. The island is now largely depopulated, with a present population of *c*.600 inhabitants. However, the remains of Norse buildings have been recorded at 30 locations, and several have been excavated, including Hamar, Sandwick, and Soterberg. These sites are difficult to date. There is a small number of accompanied burials on Unst, such as Clibberswick, with 9th-century finds. The settlements may start in that period, but many are long-lived and continue in use until the 14th and 15th centuries.

Most comprise typical Norse longhouses with wall benches and central hearths; soapstone vessels, spindle whorls, and net sinkers are common finds. As Shetland was already treeless, the timbers for the main structural beams must have been imported. At Underhoull a bow-sided hall was constructed with footings from stone recycled from an Iron Age broch and other Pictish structures. A paved floor and drain at one end suggested it had been used as a cattle byre. The extravagant use of timber for the construction of Scandinavian-style longhouses can hardly be regarded as particularly functional. Pictish architecture tended to make use of stone rather than timber. The longhouse must have been regarded as a statement of cultural identity of almost symbolic importance to the settlers, allowing them to 'feel at home' and to express a sense of community in opposition to other native communities and identities.

Associated economic changes support the idea of a Norse takeover in Orkney and Shetland. James Barrett has shown that whereas in the pre-Norse period fishing was largely a littoral activity, there was now large-scale exploitation, and an increased dietary importance of marine protein. Such fundamental changes in subsistence activity are more likely to result from large-scale colonization than from the influence of a small immigrant elite. This is particularly likely in the case of fish consumption, which was probably relatively low-status. Unlike changes in language or costume there would have been little motivation for the local population to adopt new economic practices unless this was necessitated by demographic change. This intensification of fishing must therefore have been related to the distinct cultural practices of a large immigrant population, and if not genocide, must still imply considerable population replacement.

Nonetheless, although Norse cultural traditions have retained a political importance in both the Northern and Western Isles, it would be a mistake to see them as a straight Scandinavian import. The incoming populations already demonstrate cultural mixing, and elements of indigenous culture were also retained and adapted, at least in the lower social strata. To examine the colonization of virgin territories without indigenous inhabitants we must travel further across the North Atlantic.

Chapter 10
Landnám in the North Atlantic

Viking colonization had a crucial role in shaping national identities across the North Atlantic, and Scandinavia is seen very much as the ancestral homeland. This chapter will range from the Faroes to Iceland, and from 800 to 1400, as it examines how far Viking identity and culture survived from Scandinavia and how far it was reinvented in 13th- and 14th-century sagas.

Colonization of the Faroes

The Faroes, literally 'Sheep islands', are a group of 18 islands, 290 kilometres north-west of Shetland, and 675 kilometres from the west coast of Norway. Today they have a population of *c*.45,000 which proudly preserves its Norse heritage, including the infamous whale drives. The Faroese have their own Scandinavian language, halfway between Norwegian and Icelandic. During the 19th century they began to explore their roots, looking variously to Irish hermits, Norse exiles, and Basque whalers. The leading Faroese Home Rule politician, Jóannes Patursson (1866–1946) promoted the development of Faroese archaeology, but it was Sverri Dahl (1910–87), curator of the national museum (founded 1952), who excavated the first artefact that could be attributed to the Vikings: a ringed pin from a beach-side grave at Tjørnuvik.

In 825 an Irish source, Dicuil, writing in Charlemagne's court in Aachen, finished his compilation of the most advanced geography of the time, *De Mensura Orbis Terrae*. Dicuil referred to small islands to be reached by two days' sailing north of Britain; some of these islands had been uninhabited until settled by Irish hermits. After 100 years of occupation the hermits had been driven away by pirates, although the islands were still filled with countless sheep and diverse sea birds. Although Dicuil fails to name the islands it is generally accepted that he was referring to the Faroes. The accepted wisdom, therefore, was that the Norse settlement, or *landnám*, literally land-taking, took place in the 9th century, with the small Gaelic strain in Faroese language and place names surviving from the Irish hermits.

According to the *Færeyinga Saga* (*c*.1200) the main colonization took place in the 870s when Grimur Kamban sought refuge from Haraldr Finehair of Norway. However, there is no archaeological evidence for Irish anchorites, and it has also been observed that the Gaelic element in Faroese culture cannot be a result of 8th-century hermits who should not have been in a position to have children! Another explanation for the Gaelic strain is that the original Viking settlers were first- or second-generation Norse from the Northern Isles or Ireland. At one stage pollen evidence was thought to reflect human activity *c*.650 but that has now been discredited, and the earliest dates are now *c*.875–900.

There has been little excavation on the Faroes. A Norse hall and byre were excavated at Kvívík in 1941. There was evidence for cereal cultivation and room for up to 12 cattle in the byre, but sea birds and whales were also exploited. In the 1980s, a small 10th-century settlement was excavated at Toftanes. Despite the scarcity of timber the longhouse was of typical Norse stave construction. The majority of the finds were imported, including over 700 soapstone objects, hones, quern stones, a wooden gaming board, two ringed pins, and a jet bracelet, possibly from Dublin.

14. The bay at Tjørnuvik, Faroes: site of a Norse cemetery

Early democrats or environmental catastrophe in Iceland?

Most Icelanders will tell you that their country was colonized from Norway, starting in 874, and that Ingólfr Arnarsson was the first settler. The legend says that while exploring the coast Ingólfr tossed a wooden post from his high seat into the sea and followed it until it washed ashore at what was to become the Icelandic capital at Reykjavik. Again the first colonists were said to have emigrated from Norway to escape the tyranny of Haraldr Finehair. Similarly, there were a few Irish hermits but when the Norse first arrived they soon left. At the end of the settlement period, in 930, a special law code was enacted and an open-air assembly, the Althing, was established at Thingvellir. Thus goes the origin myth of a nation that proclaims itself to be the world's first democracy, with the Althing as its first parliament.

In fact this traditional account of the Icelandic *landnám* is provided by two written sources, set down at least 300 years later, which in turn were the basis of the medieval sagas upon which 19th-century

Icelandic nationalism was founded. *Íslendingabók*, or The Book of Icelanders, was written by the priest Ari þorgilsson, (*c.*1122–33) and emphasizes the constitutional and ecclesiastical development of Iceland. *Landnámabók*, or The Book of Settlements, is an even later 13th-century source, which gives the names and histories of *c.*400 settlers. It is now seen as an attempt to give the Icelandic landscape a history combined with a post-hoc justification for medieval land-ownership patterns. It can no longer be used as an accurate description of persons and events in the 9th–11th centuries, although the Icelandic sagas based their account on it.

In reality, Iceland is closer to Scotland (795 kilometres) than it is to Norway (950 kilometres) and it is more likely that at least some of the first settlers came from the British Isles. No archaeological trace has been found of the Irish priests, or *Papar*, whom *Íslendingabók* claimed inhabited Iceland when the Norse arrived. However, modern DNA studies have revealed that approximately 20 per cent of the Icelandic gene pool probably originated in the Irish Sea region. This research has also demonstrated that while 75 per cent of male ancestors were from Scandinavia, only 37.5 per cent of females were, supporting the idea that the first colonists may have comprised a Hiberno-Norse element with Irish wives and slaves. Some place names may also relate to Norse contact with Ireland and Scotland prior to the settlement of Iceland, and there are Gaelic loan words, including the word for bull. It has even been proposed that the sagas, the heart of Icelandic identity and nationalistic feelings, actually owe their cultural roots to Irish oral poetry.

The early burials also reflect Irish influence on the costume of the early inhabitants of Iceland. Although there are 316 known pre-Christian burials, the majority were excavated in the 19th and early 20th centuries, and recorded in varying amounts of detail. Of those skeletons that can be sexed, males outnumber females by about two to one. Icelandic burials follow the general Norwegian tradition, but the graves are poorer and not at all monumental. Five boat burials are known, but all are small rowing boats used as coffins. The graves

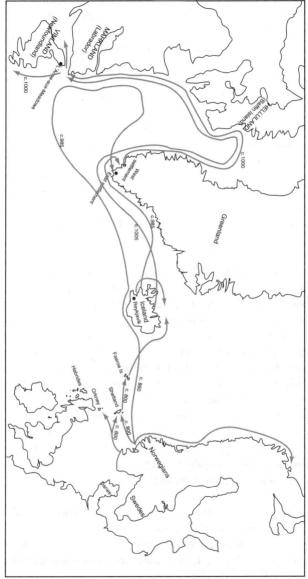

VINLAND (Newfoundland)

L'Anse-aux-Meadows

c. 1000

MARKLAND (Labrador)

HELLULAND (Baffin Island)

c. 1000

c. 985

c. 1000

Western Settlement

Eastern Settlement

c. 985

Greenland

c. 1005

Iceland

Reykjavik

Faeroe Is

c. 860

Shetland

c. 800

Hebrides

Orkney

c. 800

c. 800

Danes

Norwegians

Swedes

are generally found under low mounds located near to farms, and the majority are in small cemeteries which probably relate to family groups. As in Scotland, there is little evidence for cremation, apart from one possible burial recently excavated at Hulduholl, near Mosfell. Ornaments and weapons are found, but many graves contain only a few items, and none are rich. Unlike Scandinavia, tools are rare, suggesting a shortage of raw materials and a low calibre tool-making industry. Iron was in short supply and heavily reused. On the other hand, a high proportion of men were accompanied by their ponies, and some by dogs. Several female burials reflect the mixed cultural origin of settlers, including a woman buried with a pair of tongue-shaped brooches and a small bell at Kornsá, a second whose grave-goods included a whalebone plaque, a trefoil brooch, and a ringed pin at Hafurbjarnarstaðir, and a third at Kroppur with a ringed pin and a strap end, probably made in the British Isles.

The traditional date for the founding of Iceland in 874 has also become discredited. A number of well preserved farmsteads have been engulfed by volcanic eruptions and tephrochronology, using the ash layers as dating horizons, can provide precise chronologies. In the 1990s radiocarbon dating gave some very early dates, in the 7th and 8th centuries, but there were problems with the dates, including the likelihood that they were based on charcoal from ancient timber, and they have subsequently been discounted. On the other hand, most archaeologists now accept that settlement probably began a little before 870, with rapid and aggressive colonization leading to a drastic reduction in birch and increase in grass by 890–900, as the settlers chopped down trees and created pasture. Research has also begun to focus on the process of creation of a new society, rather than on the date of the *landnám* per se.

Landnámabok probably does give a reasonable idea of the early settlement pattern. Although Iceland has a surface area of over 103,000 square kilometres, the centre is volcanic desert, and only one-sixth is habitable. *Landnámabok* mentions 598 farmsteads, and all but 11 of these have been identified, scattered all around the coastline. It appears that the first settlers claimed large amounts of good farming land, and subsequently gave some to friends and relatives, who became their economic dependants and political followers. By the 11th century there were c.4,000 farmsteads, a figure that remained stable during the medieval and post-medieval periods. By the late 11th century the population had probably reached between 40,000 and 100,000 (compared to the present-day population of 250,000). Latecomers had to make do with slices of land in-between the large estates. Instead of being a land of isolated and independent farmers of equal status, medieval Icelandic society comprised several hundred powerful farmers each in control of a considerable number of people on his own estate and having political authority over up to 3,000 lesser farmers and cottagers bound to the estates by ties of ownership. By the 12th century, church attendance and the payment of tithes confirmed this situation.

The first farmsteads consisted of traditional longhouses, built in sod and stone, but also requiring considerable investment in timber. They had bow-sided walls with a doorway at one end and a hearth in the middle. This basic longhouse type was developed and modified, partitioned into separate rooms, and with extra rooms at the back. At Stöng, engulfed by volcanic ash in an eruption of Mt Hekla, the two additional rooms functioned as a dairy, and possibly a latrine or cold store. Such changes appear to be an adaptation to local conditions, both to the weather, so that shorter lengths of external wall were exposed, and to the growing shortage of suitable building timber.

Land ownership was the basis of economic as well as political power. Livelihoods depended upon stock-breeding, supplemented by fishing and fowling, rather than cereal cultivation. It appears that intensive colonization was accompanied by rapid environmental degradation. As the trees disappeared foraging animals had to be replaced by cows, and at Hofstaðir pigs and goats

Snorri Sturluson (1178–1241)

Snorri Sturluson was an Icelandic poet, scholar, and states-
man. From the age of 3 he studied at Oddi, the cultural
centre of Iceland. He played a leading role in politics and was
twice law-speaker at the Althing. Snorri's farm was at
Reykholt, in western Iceland. The site lies in the middle of a
wide and prosperous valley which contains some of best farm
land in Iceland. The passage-way farm has been excavated,
revealing evidence for at least two important activity areas:
wool-processing and de-lousing! Some cereal grain was also
found, but must have been imported from Europe. Snorri's
career brought him many enemies, including King Hákon
of Norway, who had him killed in the cellar at Reykholt,
in 1241.

Snorri's importance today rests upon his literary works. He
compiled *Heimskringla*, a history of the Norse kings, which
despite including a mythological section based on sagas, is
also a key source for the early history of Iceland and Norway.
Snorri was the author of the *Prose Edda*, which preserves
fragments of 10th-century skaldic poetry, and may also have
written *Egils Saga*.

decline in proportion to cattle during the 10th century. However,
cattle had to be kept indoors for much of the year, their survival
dependent upon the availability of fodder. At Svalbarð, in north-
east Iceland, sheep herding was important from the first phase but,
as the climate declines when Europe entered the Little Ice Age,
sealing also became more important. At Svalbarð there was no
cereal grain although hay was gathered for fodder and to cover the
floor, and peat was used for bedding, fuel, and construction. Wild

berries, such as bilberry and crowberry, and edible seeds and leaves were also collected.

In academic discussions of early Iceland the previous focus on *landnám* and settlement origins has been replaced by a more modern 21st-century theme of environmental disaster. It has been estimated that 60 per cent of the original natural vegetation cover of Iceland was destroyed due to woodland clearance and over-grazing, followed by soil erosion. Landscape degradation enhanced by cooling climatic conditions subjected the Viking cultural system to severe stress – in economic, demographic, and social structures. In a society where families had become dispersed because of migration, new systems, such as *hreppur* – or agricultural cooperatives – had to replace former familial safeguards with a form of social services.

In summary, in the North Atlantic colonies, cultural change was eventually determined by environmental factors rather than by hybridization with an existing population, although the incoming colonists were by no means pure Scandinavian stock in the first place. The attachment to a Viking cultural identity was as much as a creation of later origin myths, at a time when it was politically expedient to look to a shared Scandinavian homeland.

Chapter 11

The edge of the world: Greenland and North America

Greenland was the most isolated of the Viking colonies and had the most extreme environment. The story of its foundation has again been derived from later written sources, principally the *Íslendingabók* (1122–32). This recounts how Eirik the Red, on a three-year exile from Iceland, reconnoitred the west coast in 981–2. Three years later he persuaded 300 Icelanders to return with him in 25 ships; only 14 ships made it. The colonists split into two groups: the larger group under Eirik settled on the south-west coast in what became known as the Eastern Settlement; a second group sailed 650 kilometres north along an inhospitable coastline before making landfall and founding the Western Settlement.

From the 11th to 12th centuries written sources mention some 190 farms in the Eastern Settlement, and a further 90 in the Western. There may have been somewhere between 2,000 and 4,000 people living on Greenland at the height of the colonies; over their total lifespan it has been suggested that *c.*25,000–35,000 settlers lived there. Given the absence of later occupation, the Norse settlement pattern is well preserved; *c.*250 farms and

20 churches have been identified archaeologically. In order to maximize the available grazing the farms are dispersed, as in Iceland, usually several kilometres apart and separated by mountains and swamps. Cereal cultivation was impossible; domestic animals were kept, but much energy was expended on gathering winter fodder as the cattle had to be kept indoors all winter. By the end of winter in April the farms would have been under severe stress. To supplement their diet the Greenlanders grew to depend on seals, which make up 35–70 per cent of bones found. Each of the farms invested some of their seal meat in keeping great dogs alive. These may have been used for herding sheep, and as guard dogs, but they may represent the lord's hunting pack, split up amongst the farms to keep them fed over winter, but brought together to hunt caribou in the summer. The Greenlanders also traded skins and ivory with Iceland and Europe to obtain grain, salt, and iron.

Excavations in the 1990s at a well preserved Western Settlement farm complex at Gård Under Sandet (or GUS) have revealed what a typical Greenlandic farm might have been like. The farm had been established *c.*1000, and was occupied through a series of rebuildings until *c.*1350. It comprised some 38 rooms, of which 12 were still in use in the final phase of occupation. They were built of timber, including driftwood and fresh timber – much of which must have been imported from Vinland, Siberia, or Norway. The buildings had pitched timber roofs, their underside lined with branches for insulation, and covered with turf on the exterior. Despite the survival of wood in the permafrost no furniture was found, suggesting that the last occupants took their most useful belongings with them. Sheep were kept for wool; goats and cows supplied milk, which was kept in barrels. Hare, seal, and caribou were hunted, and fibres from bison and brown bear fur, recovered in a 14th-century weaving room, suggest that these Greenlanders travelled to North America.

Eirik the Red (*c.*950–1003)

Eirik is the archetypal Viking: a bold leader, aggressive, pioneering, a visionary democrat, good husband, proud father, and red-haired. According to *Eirik's Saga*, he was born in Norway but his family was forced to flee to Iceland when his father, Thorvald Asvaldsson, was exiled because of a murder. In 981–2 Eirik had to flee again because of another murder and he spent three years in outlawry exploring the coast of Greenland. In 984–5 he returned and built the estate Brattahlid, or 'steep slope', in the Eastern Settlement. Eirik's title was that of 'paramount chieftain'. His farm is presumed to lie under Qassiarsuk where a large farm and church were excavated in 1932. The church has been interpreted as that built by Eirik's wife, Thjodhild, who moved out once she became Christian. Eirik died in 1003, having fallen victim to an epidemic brought by a fresh group of immigrants. According to the sagas, Eirik had four children: a daughter, Freydis, as well as three sons, Thorvald, and Thorsteinn, and the explorer Leif Eiriksson.

To boldly go: Vikings in North America

The idea that Vikings discovered America, some 500 years before Columbus, and there encountered strange savages, appeals to the modern quest for adventure, and has been given a contemporary resonance in the exploration of space, and its fictional counterpart in the TV series *Star Trek*. Unfortunately the archaeological evidence is limited, and some of it has been invented. The narrative of the discovery of America is based upon stories first recorded in the sagas, some 200 years after the event. These were originally read as objective historical documents; then dismissed as medieval fantasy. The current view lies somewhere in between; the sagas probably preserve elements of fact but are likely to have embellished and conflated events. The story of the discovery of America probably represents a semi-mythological account of a sequence of exploration and contact that continued over several decades.

The two primary accounts, in *Greenlanders' Saga* (*c.*1200) and *Eirik's Saga* (*c.*1210–30), appear to have been based on the same original material but diverge substantially. In *Greenlanders' Saga*, Vinland is discovered in two stages. Bjarni Herjolfsson, on his way from Norway to Greenland, is blown off course and accidentally discovers unknown lands south-west of Greenland. Later, in *c.*1000, Eirik the Red's son, Leif, sets out with the aim of exploring the land seen by Bjarni. He visits new areas and names them Helluland, Markland, and Vinland, establishing his base in the latter location. Leif Eirikson then over-winters with his crew before returning to Greenland the following spring. His brother Thorvald returns and explores the coast, but encounters hostile natives, and in a bloody skirmish is killed by an arrow. In *Eirik's Saga*, on the other hand, no mention is made of Bjarni and it is Leif who is blown off course and first sets foot ashore. Exploration of the new lands is credited to Thorfinn Karlsefni, an Icelandic trader, but after three winters, harassed by native Indians, his party returned home.

The location of Vinland has been much debated. Interpretations range from Labrador to Florida, but the consensus is Newfoundland. Vinland is named as the most southerly of the lands encountered and Helluland may be Baffin Island, making Markland Central Labrador. The name Vinland is problematic. It is mentioned in 1075 by Adam of Bremen, specifically as derived from the presence of wild grapes, which do not grow on Newfoundland. However, it is possible that Adam made a mistake and it was the Norse word *vinland* with a short, not long 'i', meaning 'natural meadow or pasture'. Alternatively it has been argued that, as there are wild grapes in the New Brunswick or St Lawrence River area, these resources were certainly available.

Newfoundland's claim to be Vinland became stronger in the 1960s with the discovery of L'Anse aux Meadows, situated on its northernmost tip. The site provided the first clear archaeological proof that the Vikings reached North America. A small Norse settlement was located on a narrow terrace, cut by a small brook. Three types of building have been identified. Three large multi-roomed halls are distinctively Icelandic in shape and layout. They have traits which were common at the end of the 10th century, but lack details developed after the 11th century. The halls each contained one or more rooms where people ate, slept, and socialized. Each of these rooms had a hearth in the centre with wall benches along the sides; each also contained a workshop and a large storage room. It has been suggested that goods were being collected here for trans-shipment, including nuts, grapes, and fine hardwood. Butternuts found in the floor layers are not local and must have come from the area of Quebec or New Brunswick.

Three smaller pit buildings appear to be paired with the halls. As they contained fireplaces they may have been used as accommodation, possibly for slaves, but the presence of 19 net sinkers in one of the huts suggests this was used as a fishing gear store. One of the larger halls also had a smaller rectangular house, of a type used on elite farms for subordinate labour, built next to it. On the far side of the brook away from the buildings there was a bloomery, comprising a simple iron-smelting furnace, with a charcoal kiln nearby. Iron smelting was unknown to the native peoples who inhabited this area and radiocarbon dates from Norse rubbish layers give a 95 per cent probability that the site was occupied between 990–1030. There is evidence for earlier and later Indian occupation at L'Anse, but no evidence for contemporaneity or overlap.

From the size of the bench sleeping space in the living quarters it has been estimated that the halls could accommodate 77–92 people in total. The two largest halls each also had a private chamber at one end, of a type used by manor owners on Iceland. The grouping of

16. L'Anse aux Meadows reconstruction

the buildings into three complexes may suggest three ship's crews, each of around 30 individuals. However, the small size of the rubbish middens and the lack of evidence for building repair suggests occupation was short-lived, although the site must have been intended for year-round occupation as the buildings were solid structures rather than booths. There are no byres, stables, or animal pens, and no cemetery. There were no domestic food bones; the meat consumed was primarily seal and whale. Abandonment was deliberate and orderly with very little material left behind. Only a small number of personal items were recovered and the finds mainly comprised waste associated with either building construction or boat repair, including some 3 kg of iron waste, smithing slag, discarded rivets, and carpentry debris, including a patch, possibly for a small boat.

It seems reasonable to conclude that L'Anse aux Meadows may be the site mentioned in the sagas as settled by Leif. Only a chieftain such as Leif could establish a site like this, and the scale of operations makes it unlikely that it is an unnamed settlement, especially given the effort that must have gone into its construction. At the time it was built the total population of Greenland was only $c.2,500$. If the estimates are correct then L'Anse aux Meadows was occupied by 10–20 per cent of the population of the entire Greenland colony, presumably mostly by men of prime working age. It seems highly unlikely that the Norse had sufficient resources to construct a string of such settlements.

L'Anse aux Meadows could certainly have functioned as a gateway site. The long distance from Greenland to southern resources in America means this is a good spot for over-wintering, allowing the collection of resources before return. The journey from Brattahlid to L'Anse is over 3,000 kilometres; such a voyage would take perhaps a month, leaving only one or two months for exploration as travel would only have been possible from June to September. The site thus probably belongs to the period when the Greenland colony was exploring and assessing what resources were available. However, it had no long-term viability, because of a number of factors, including the great distances and treacherous seas, the threat of hostile natives, the lack of resources at L'Anse, and the fact that desirable resources were so far away that they were not worth the labour and time required. Lumber and wine could be had from Europe, which also had more to offer in way of luxuries, food, family ties, and the church. In comparison with Europe, the New World had little to recommend it. The Greenland settlement was itself too small to be able to afford a splinter colony and either all had to go to Vinland, or none. When the decision was taken to abandon L'Anse aux Meadows, the North American adventure was abandoned with it.

Given the distances already travelled across the North Atlantic compared with the distance involved from Newfoundland to Greenland, it is perhaps unsurprising that the Norse made landfall in North America. But apart from the effect on the modern American psyche, did their visits have any lasting effects on the native peoples? Both *Eirik's Saga* and the *Greenlanders' Saga* describe episodes of peaceful trading between Norse and natives, and in *Eirik's Saga* Karlsefni and his men trade red cloth for pelts. While there is no North American site where direct contact can be demonstrated, the quantity and distribution of Norse finds on native sites indicates more contact than recorded in the sagas, and overall the material is consistent with wide-ranging but sporadic contact, rather than long-distance trading of Norse goods obtained by raiding in Greenland. Despite this there was very little cultural borrowing. The cultures were completely alien to each other and evidently neither felt it had anything to gain by copying the other's technology or behaviour.

Decline and abandonment

The timing of, and reasons for, the abandonment of the Greenland colonies have been much debated. These questions have taken on an importance partly because the colonies represent an unusual Viking failure, and with it, the end of Scandinavian expansion westwards. In 1497 Newfoundland was 'rediscovered' by John Cabot. Was there a real gap in European knowledge of the North Atlantic in-between?

Ivar Bardarson, a cleric from Trondheim, came to Greenland in the 1340s to administer the church from Garðar. When he returned to Norway he reported that by the mid-1350s nothing had been heard from the Western Settlement for several years. Bardarson mounted an expedition to investigate, but his ship found abandoned farms, the animals half-wild, with no trace of any inhabitants. The Western Settlement is therefore believed to have come to a close in the mid-14th century. The last documentary reference to the Eastern Settlement comes from accounts of an Icelandic ship beset by storms and fog during a 1406 voyage from Norway, driven to Greenland. The crew lived among the farmers of the Eastern Settlement for four years, and one of them was married in the stone church in Hvalsey. When they sailed for Norway in 1410 that was the last that anyone heard of the settlement, which is thought to have died out by 1450.

Several reasons have been suggested for the failure of the colonies. One suggestion is that climatic deterioration changed the migratory routes of the caribou, while the settlers were tied to one place by their domestic animals. Grazing deteriorated and the west coast was sealed off from Europe. However, the evidence is inconclusive and for modern scholars such environmental determinism is seen as too simplistic. The Little Ice Age is unlikely to have destroyed the Norse colonists – the intensive chill did not take place before 1600 – by which time they had already disappeared. On the other hand, the observed decline in vegetation may have been caused by the Norse by over-grazing.

Second, it has been argued that the Greenlanders suffered from disease and malnutrition, and may even have been wiped out by the Black Death. However, apart from revealing an increased reliance on marine species, all the skeletons that have been analysed are healthy.

The breakdown of trade with Europe certainly was important. By the 14th century elephant ivory from India and furs from Russia were readily available and the economic basis of the colony was thus undermined.

Fourth, the failure has been blamed on increased competition with the Inuit. The late 13th-/early 14th-century *Historia Norvegiae* recorded violent contact between Norse hunters and *skraelings* who 'used walrus teeth for missiles and sharpened stones for knives', although few now believe that Inuit attacks can have been the sole reason for Norse depopulation, and their arrival in the Western Settlement may well have been after it was already deserted. It is, however, significant that Inuit artefacts and technology are conspicuously absent from Norse sites. The Norse did not adopt Inuit skin-covered umiaks and kayaks, or their clothing styles; nor did they acquire harpoon-hunting technology to widen their subsistence base.

Lack of adaptation certainly seems to have been an important factor in the Norse decline. Norse farmers were tied to isolated pockets of pasture capable of supporting domestic animals. They took little advantage of the sea; even seals were only clubbed when they came on land, whereas the Inuit hunted them by boat. Farmers lived in a stratified society controlled by powerful chieftains and church officials. The social and economic structure rested upon payment of tithes to landowners, the church, and the Norwegian crown.

The church was an important influence: over 20 local churches were constructed, replete with stained glass, bells, and vestments. Its main power centre was at Garðar where a bishopric was established on the rim of the known world and a small stone cathedral was dedicated to St Nicholas. The bishop's palace complex included a tithe barn where the skulls of 25 walrus and five narwhal skulls indicate the level of tithes. Two huge cow byres with space for 150 cattle show the concentration of economic power. Analysis of the bishop's skeleton (identified by his crosier) revealed that he – unlike his parishioners – was able to live off a diet of land animals, rather than seal meat. In 2000 Thomas McGovern attributed the failure of the Greenland colony to a single-minded concentration on European-style stock-raising strategies:

> When faced with multiple challenges to the basic environmental and social framework of their economy and society, the Norse Greenlanders chose to avoid innovation, to emphasize and elaborate their own traditions, and ultimately to die rather than abandon what they must have seen as core values.

Several sites provide evocative archaeological evidence for the end of the Norse colonies. At the bishop's palace at Garðar nine partial skeletons of hunting dogs lay on floors of stables and dwelling houses, buried beneath collapsing roof timbers in the mid-14th century. At GUS, the farm was abandoned at around the same time. A solitary goat later returned, and with no one left to care for him, starved to death outside. Later still, after the roof had partially collapsed, a group of Inuit came and camped in the abandoned farmstead, but their fire set the ruins alight and they fled, leaving behind some of their belongings. At Site W54, adjacent to GUS, bio-archaeology has revealed the death of the farmstead, as warmth-loving insects in the lower farm levels were replaced by carrion-loving insects in the upper layers. All that was left in the larder were cattle hooves, mixed with the feet of ptarmigan and arctic hare. In the hallway outside the larder was the partial skeleton of one of the great hunting dogs. Cut marks to the bones revealed that this faithful hound had provided the last supper of the occupants.

This poignant tale of starving 14th-century settlers, clinging to a maladaptive lifestyle, is a far cry from warrior-kings of the 9th-century, and emphasizes the wide range of cultural behaviour to which the term Viking has been applied. In the last chapter it is time to return to the issue of how these different roles have been taken up by subsequent commentators and been used to create their own Vikings.

Chapter 12
Reinventing the Vikings

At the outset of this book I observed that 'Viking' was not a common term in the 9th and 10th centuries, and that our modern image probably owes more to recent appropriation of the term than to any historically-based reality. In subsequent chapters we have looked at what archaeology can tell us about the cultural identities of those peoples who lived in Scandinavia and its colonies during what we now call the Viking Age. But every age has reinvented the Vikings and in this chapter we will examine some of these more recent reinventions.

Nineteenth-century Vikings – the Romantic revival

By the 16th century there was scant appreciation of Scandinavia's early history, and knowledge of the Viking Age was virtually non-existent. Despite Ole Worm's catalogue of Danish monuments, *Danicorum Monumentorum* (1643), scholarly interest was limited. Europeans were more concerned with their classical past and the great civilizations of Greece and Rome. From the late 18th century, however, Vikings began to become fashionable again, not as cultural heroes, but exactly because they were considered barbarians. Vikings and other early medieval cultures provided indigenous European examples of Rousseau's 'Noble Savage'.

This new enthusiasm for Vikings became particularly intense in

Denmark and Sweden after both countries suffered humiliating military defeats. In 1807 Nelson bombarded Copenhagen; in 1809 Sweden lost Finland to Russia. With the conclusion of the Napoleonic Wars patriotic romanticism grew in many countries. In Scandinavia, the educated classes felt the need to recover the power and vitality of the Viking Age. Vikings became core to their maintenance of a sense of national identity. In 1808 Nikolai Grundtvig's *Northern Mythology* was published in Denmark. Grundtvig (1783–1872) campaigned to infuse the Danish education system with the Viking spirit. Today he is widely regarded as the founder of lifelong learning. Grundtvig retold the Viking myths in the form of a chronology of the sagas, the aim of which was to develop the prestige of Scandinavia in Europe. In 1811 the Gothic Society was founded in Sweden. Its purpose was to encourage the patriotic spirit and encourage archaeological research. An all-male group, its anthem was 'In ancient times Goths drank from horns'. Drinking horns were given pride of place in middle-class dining rooms throughout Scandinavia. Its members included Erik Gustaf Geijer, whose poem *The Viking* portrayed an ideal society where harmony depended on the balance between free farmers and high kings, and Esaias Tegnér, author of the poetic romance *Frithiofs Saga*.

While poets and students met to read Old Norse songs and poems, they looked to archaeology for a Viking Age that could be displayed. Burial mounds were obvious man-made features and were targeted for investigation. One of the royal mounds at Jelling was dug in 1820; the second in 1861. The three great mounds at Old Uppsala were dug in 1846–7 and 1874; in 1852 the Borre ship burial was excavated. From 1873–95 Stolpe excavated over 1,000 graves at Birka. At about this time the term 'Viking Age' was used for the first time in Scandinavia by Oscar Montelius, to refer to the period 800–1050.

At the same time as agricultural improvements and deep ploughing were leading to a rapid increase in the pace of archaeological discoveries in Scandinavia, industrialization and urban growth were creating an urban proletariat who saw themselves as Swedish or Danish rather than as the inhabitants of local farming districts. Norway was part of Denmark up to 1814; then it became part of Sweden until achieving independence in 1905. Nationalism was particularly intense and regional dialect studies were taken as proof of a greater Norwegian affinity with their Viking heritage and Old Norse than with either Denmark or Sweden.

In summary, the image of the Vikings in 19th-century Scandinavia was characterized by a number of features, several of which have had lasting impact. First, a homogeneous Viking Age culture was identified in Scandinavia, lasting from 800 to 1050. This Viking Age was seen as a step on the evolutionary ladder, equivalent to those of Stone, Bronze, and Iron in a grand Darwinian perspective. The Viking past was owned solely by the Scandinavian nations and the key historical actors were the early Viking kings, particularly those involved in unification. Where possible, their history should be written from documentary sources, and illustrated by archaeological finds. Its main themes were political unification, Viking voyages, and the process of conversion to Christianity. By the 20th century the Vikings had become one of a small number of 'great civilizations', and interest focused on the rise of the Scandinavian states. However, differences between regions were secondary to a shared common culture and language, visible in the archaeological evidence.

Outside Scandinavia, Vikings were also taken initially to represent pre-classical barbarian culture, but the romantic appeal of the sagas soon became combined with the revival of interest in the northern world and the search for northern 'primitive' ancestors.

In Britain the Vikings were reinvented in accordance with Victorian notions of race, valour, and enterprise. Comparisons were drawn between the Viking spirit and the enterprising spirit of Victorian entrepreneurs and explorers. Old Norse and Anglo-Saxon were revived as university subjects equal to the classical languages, and chairs were endowed particularly in northern industrial towns,

Richard Wagner (1813–83) . . . and horned helmets

Richard Wagner used a series of sagas and other sources when he composed *The Ring of the Nibelung*, first performed 1869–76. Reworking his Norse sources, Wagner combined two stories: the tale of Sigurd and the account of *Ragnarök*, the downfall of the Norse gods, to create a pastiche of Germanic and Scandinavian mythology. He is often credited with popularizing the idea of horned helmets, giving one to the character Hunding in the Ring cycle. In later productions horned helmets were most closely associated with the Valkyries, but as originally staged the Valkyries wore helmets with wings. Wagner and his costume and set designer Carl Emil Doepler probably borrowed the idea from the costumes in stage plays about ancient pre-Viking Germans, and used it in the original production of *Tristan und Isolde* in 1865.

In fact Vikings first acquired horned and winged helmets during the 19th century. Romantic artists began to explore mythology, depicting a hodgepodge of Germanic, Celtic, and classical motifs. The Swede Gustav Malmström gave horns to Vikings in illustrations for an edition of *Frithiof's Saga* (1820–5), but may have borrowed the idea from prehistoric Scandinavian rock art. There are depictions of horned figures in the Viking Age, on a tapestry from the Oseberg ship burial, but they are shamanistic figures in a ceremonial procession. The only surviving horned helmet is Iron Age, dredged from the Thames at Waterloo Bridge in the 1860s, and now in the British Museum. Some Viking warriors did wear helmets in battle, but they were simple conical affairs, such as that found at Gjermundbu, in Sweden, or that depicted on the Middleton cross.

such as Manchester and Leeds. Victorian writers also fuelled the popular interest, and the Pre-Raphaelites turned away from classical to Norse and Germanic heroes. Even the landscape was appropriated and for them the Lake District was a Viking landscape, frozen in time. In 1892 the Viking Society for Northern Research was founded, and began the publication of *Sagabook*, the first periodical devoted to the study of Vikings. There was particular interest in the links between Germanic myth and Christian teaching, which encouraged the study of Viking sculpture as it depicted events in heathen mythology alongside Christian scenes in ways which emphasized the parallels.

William Morris (1834–96)

William Morris, designer, author, and revolutionary social-ist, developed a passion for medieval Scandinavia while an undergraduate at Oxford. Morris identified with the Norse heroes and learnt Icelandic from Eiríkr Magnússon, with whom he translated a number of sagas. His two voyages to Iceland, in 1871 and 1873, were highly influential on his art, poetry, and politics. His Icelandic epic poem, *Sigurd the Volsung*, was published in 1876. Morris's friends in the Pre-Raphaelite movement, particularly Burne-Jones and Ford Madox Brown, also had romantic Viking themes in their paintings. For Morris, however, the Norsemen were hard-working socialists. As a founding member of the Socialist League, Morris was at the centre of political unrest in Britain in 1886–7. His visionary novel *News from Nowhere* became an essential socialist text and his influence runs down to Clement Atlee and the post-war welfare state. As late as the 1970s his views on the environment led him to be recognized as a founding father of green politics too.

William Collingwood (1854–1932)

As a student reading Greats at Oxford, William Collingwood came under the patronage of John Ruskin. After studying at the Slade between 1876 and 1878, he became a research assistant and secretary to Ruskin, travelling with him, and living close by in Coniston. During the 1890s Collingwood developed his painting skills but also published regularly in the Transactions of the Cumberland and Westmorland Antiquarian and Archaeological Society, of which he was to become Editor and then President. Collingwood was drawn to Norse legend and felt that the Lake District represented a Norse landscape. He wrote a series of novels, including *Thorstein of the Mere* (1895) and *The Bondwoman* (1896) set against that background. In 1897 he visited Iceland and later published, with Jon Stefansson, his *Pilgrimage to the Sagasteads of Iceland*. He was a member of the Viking Club, and served as its president. He became particularly interested in the artistic aspects of Norse culture in England, and devoted himself to drawing and cataloguing the stone sculpture. This was published shortly before his death as *Northumbrian Crosses of the pre-Norman Age* (1927), perhaps his most important work.

Sir Walter Scott was fascinated by the Norse history of Scotland and set the opening scene of his novel *The Pirate* (1828) at the Shetland site he christened Jarlshof. A host of children's books were published, notably Ballantine's *Erling the Bold* (1869) and Sabine Baring-Gould's *Grettir the Outlaw* (1890). Meanwhile historians were also writing academic books on Vikings. In 1841 Thomas Carlyle published *On Heroes, Hero-Worship and the Heroic in History* in which he saw Oðinn as the emblem of the strong inspired leader, and in 1875 he produced *The Early Kings of Norway*.

In general, however, when Vikings were described by English historians, they often appeared as treacherous barbarians, and as foils for the great hero King Ælfred. It is not surprising that the German-speaking rulers of Great Britain and their supporters should look to the Anglo-Saxons as their forebears. For the English, then as now, the Anglo-Saxons were the ancestral *us*, while the Vikings were *them*. The Scandinavians only settled in part of England and the subsequent 'reconquest' made the whole episode seem like a temporary blip in the development of a unified English kingdom and, unlike the Norman Conquest, the Viking invasions created no long-term constitutional changes.

Furthermore, the Vikings in England failed to produce a historian; their deeds were known solely through the eyes of the West Saxon chroniclers, and so long as later historians accepted this propaganda as fact, the Vikings were guaranteed short shrift. It was Ælfred, Victorian school children were taught, who unified the nation, saved the English from the invaders, and founded the British Navy, while mixing with the common people with ease, despite burning their cakes. On the other hand, the Vikings had also to be portrayed as worthy adversaries, and by the end of the 19th century were almost seen as benefactors of the lands they raided. They were equated with nobility of adventure and in many places were seen as the founders of democracy.

Vikings and Nazis

In Germany under the Nazis a more sinister interpretation of Vikings developed. During the late 19th century Wagnerian mystique was merged with Nietzsche's elitist philosophy of the superman. Some Germans began to see themselves as the *Herrenwolk*, or master race. Vikings became their own racial forebears and role models, destined to defeat their inferiors in other countries.

After Germany's humiliating defeat in the First World War, these ideas were turned into party politics by Hitler and his followers. The Nazis attempted to close ranks with the so-called Aryan people of Scandinavia. When they came to power in 1933 they began a crusade against modern 'decadent' culture, systematically replacing it with their own version of Aryan culture, based on Vikings, Old Norse mythology, Wagner, and German peasant culture. The Vikings became part of the fair-haired, blue-eyed, clean-living ideal of the National Socialist Party. At its most extreme, Nazism intended to replace Christianity with the old paganism of the Germanic gods. The excavations at Hedeby in the 1930s were strongly backed by the political apparatus of the German state, which wished to emphasize a unity with the people of Scandinavia which had little foundation in reality.

Similar ideals were adopted by right-wing groups in the Scandinavian countries. The Norwegian National Socialist party used the barrow cemetery at Borre, Vestfold, in Norway, as a backdrop for political rallies from 1935 to 1944:

> We gather here because the people who united Norway in one kingdom were buried here. These people carried the name of Norway all over the world. It was these people who founded states in Russia and, in a certain sense, also the British Empire.

Northern European Neo-Nazi groups continue to seek intellectual justification by perverting aspects of pre-Christian religious beliefs and appropriating Viking sites, notably those with ceremonial associations, such as Old Uppsala.

Fakes and forgeries in the United States

Amongst many of the modern inhabitants of North America the quest for European ancestry is an important part of their cultural identity. Many have seized upon finds that purport to show pre-Columbian European settlement, and some have not stopped short of inventing them.

17. Second World War recruitment poster

In 1879 a Swedish emigrant arrived in Douglas County in Minnesota and settled in the town of Kensington. In 1898 he announced that when digging deep in his fields he had found a large rune stone, *c.*0.8m in height, between the roots of a large poplar tree. The text purported to say:

> 8 Goths and 22 Norwegians on a voyage of exploration west of Vinland. One day's journey north of this stone we camped close to two rocky inlets. One day we went out fishing and on our return found the dead bodies of ten of our men, red with blood. AVM deliver us from evil. 14 days journey away from this island, then men are keeping watch over our ships. 1362.

Prominent Scandinavian and American runologists immediately declared it to be a fake as the runes were nonsense. Nonetheless it was exhibited in the Smithsonian Museum as a genuine artefact in 1948–53. By 1950 no fewer than 24 runic inscriptions were cited as evidence for Norse settlement in North America. Subsequently the Kensington runes were proved to have been carved with a chisel of a type sold in Minnesota at the end of last century and the farmer was found to be an amateur runologist with a collection of books on runes. The Runestone Museum in Alexandria, however, still features the Kensington stone as its prize exhibit.

The authenticity of the so-called Vinland map has been even more bitterly contested. The map was published by Yale University in 1965, having been bought on their behalf, reputedly for one million dollars. It comprises a pen and ink map of the world on thin parchment. The representation of the Old World is consistent with maps of the Middle Ages, and follows the custom of placing some fictional islands in the Atlantic. It also includes, however, two large islands in the North Atlantic: Greenland, and a second island labelled 'Vinland, discovered by Bjarni and Leif in company'. The map was supposedly created in Germany or Switzerland, probably in association with the Council of Basle, which met 1431–49.

In fact, there are several reasons for regarding it as a forgery. First, Greenland is depicted as an island, although this was not discovered until 1902. Second, the depiction of the eastern North Atlantic is

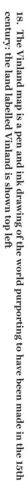
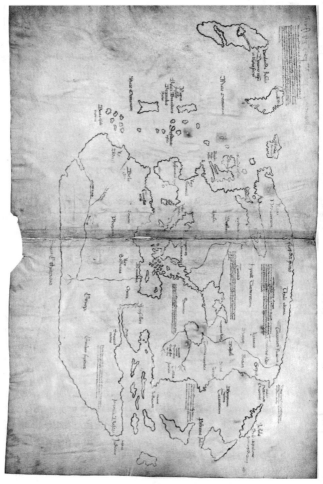

18. The Vinland map is a pen and ink drawing of the world purporting to have been made in the 15th century: the land labelled Vinland is shown top left

based upon 16th-century Portuguese maps that only gained public attention in the late 19th century. Finally, the ink was tested in a Chicago laboratory and found to contain titanium pigment not available before 1917 at the earliest. In fact, this ink is now falling off the map. However, like all good forgeries the Vinland map has refused to go away. In 1986 the ink was reanalysed at the University of California. There it was declared that only microscopic amounts of titanium were present and that both ink and parchment were consistent with a 15th-century origin. One of the interesting features of both the Kensington rune stone and the Vinland map is that, for those people who want to believe in them, scientific evidence can be dismissed as unimportant, or beaten into submission.

As is generally the case in the writing of history there are political undertones to all of this. Earlier attempts to find ancestral Europeans in America did so at the expense of native North Americans. Indigenous monumental architectural achievements could not be accepted as the product of barbarian cultures which had been all but exterminated by the white man, and it was important to establish a prior claim for 19th-century settlers. Stone structures and burial mounds were cited as evidence of Viking activity, rather than accepted as the work of a sophisticated palaeo-indian or Inuit culture. Scandinavian finds were found further and further down the eastern seaboard of the United States, although they were still concentrated in areas of high 19th-century Scandinavian immigration.

Today the message has changed, but is just as loaded. Despite the fact that the only attested Viking site is at L'Anse aux Meadows (p. 110), firmly in Canada, in 2000 the Smithsonian Institution in Washington staged a major Viking exhibition, to mark the 1000th anniversary of Leif Eriksson's historic voyage. The preface to the book which accompanied the exhibition (Fitzhugh and Ward 2000) was by Hilary Clinton. The First Lady noted that Viking women were active participants in politics and religion, while the disappearance of the Norse on Greenland may have been a consequence of poor environmental management. The volume editors accepted the lack of evidence for long-term Viking settlement in America, but noted that (p. 24):

> Perhaps the most important outcome of contact was the familiarity Native Americans gained about European habits, behavior, and materials which helped them take best advantage of future interactions.

Jorvik, DNA, and Vikings today

In the 21st century, in Europe, Scandinavia, and North America, the Vikings carry huge popular interest: they sell books and television programmes, advertise goods, and persuade people to visit museums. When the decision was taken to create a new type of museum in York, the subject chosen was not Romans or Anglo-Saxons, but Vikings. When it opened in 1984, the Jorvik Viking Centre attracted over 800,000 visitors in its first year, taking it into the top three tourist attractions. Shortly after Jorvik was reopened by Tony Blair in 2001, following a £4 million facelift, the 12 millionth customer passed through the door. Visitors are now invited to go back in time and travel through 10th-century Jorvik in suspended time capsules, for the 'authentic Viking encounter'. With ambient sound systems, directional aerosol sprays, and robotic chickens, this is a truly 21st-century Viking experience.

For those seeking a more active Viking lifestyle, re-enactment groups have flourished in Europe, Scandinavia, and North America. These cater for all tastes, from those with an eye for detail and rigorous policing against any anachronistic costume items, to those which just provide a legal excuse for a good fight, and even some which combine both. For the descendants of 'Briese-Bane' (or bone-breaker) there is even an active Viking re-enactment group in Queensland, Australia. Although some groups initially focused upon the Viking warrior and raider stereotype, they have moved

19. **Street scene, Jorvik**

with the times and now have Viking camps in which traders and craftsmen, women and children, are welcome. In Britain, The Vikings, originally founded in 1971 as the Norse Film and Pageant Society, is the oldest Dark Age re-enactment group. They regularly appear at English Heritage sites, and as battle extras in films and TV documentaries. Membership is rigidly stratified, as *unfree thralls*, *fri-halls*, *drengr*, and *jarls*. The society has a membership of over 600, and its own website at www.vikingsonline.org.uk!

Another way in which Vikings have taken over leisure time is though metal-detecting. In eastern England and some parts of Scandinavia this popular hobby has begun to provide evidence for dense Viking Age settlement. Official schemes to record finds are now starting to put some of this information into the public domain (www.finds.org.uk). Some metal-detectorists are no doubt motivated by financial gain, which has brought them into conflict with archaeologists, but many took up the hobby because of a genuine interest in the past.

Other people believe that they are Vikings or are descended from Vikings. DNA research has raised misguided expectations that it might be possible to identify a Viking gene and I occasionally receive letters and email messages from those whose hair colour, family name, or temperament leads them to believe that they are the direct descendants of Viking settlers. In fact it is very hard to say anything about individuals from their DNA, although stronger statements can be made about populations. Identifying Vikings from hair colour or skull shape is even more unreliable, as physical characteristics bear only an approximation to genes, and environment can be an important factor, although blood groups provide a closer proxy for DNA.

A major genetics survey carried out for the BBC in 2001 took DNA samples from men at a number of sites. In the main, small towns were chosen and the men tested were required to be able to trace their male line back two generations in the same rural area. The aim was to reduce the effects of later population movements, assuming that in-between the Norman invasion of 1066 and the 20th century movement would have been limited. The tests looked at the Y chromosome, which is only carried by men. Samples taken in modern-day Norway were used to represent the Norwegian Vikings, and samples from Denmark represented the Danish input. The results were disappointing but probably not surprising. Eastern England has been subject to invasion from adjacent areas of the continental mainland for countless millennia. Some migrations are historically attested although the majority, going back into prehistory, are undocumented. In England the survey team encountered difficulties in distinguishing between the DNA of Saxon and Danish invaders. The outlying Scottish isles provided the most conclusive evidence of a Scandinavian presence. In the Northern and Western Isles, as well as in the far north of the Scottish mainland, Norwegian genetic signatures were found. In

Shetland and Orkney 60 per cent of the male population had DNA of Norwegian origin, although again it is very difficult to establish the date that this was transmitted from modern populations. Other research has found that the DNA of the modern-day populations of the Central Lakes and north-east Derbyshire differs from that of the surrounding areas, in a way that is much closer to that of Denmark.

Attempts have been made to extract ancient DNA from excavated human remains, but there are great risks of contamination. Indeed, results of a recent test appeared to show that a Viking warrior from Repton had come from Africa! Techniques are still being refined but for the present they may be unreliable. Oxygen and strontium isotope analysis of teeth appears to be more promising. Put crudely, we are what we drink, and the chemical composition of the water consumed in childhood is preserved in our teeth. Given the distinctive geology of some areas, including Norway, it is possible to define a fingerprint for the local water, making it possible to identify those who grew up there, such as the Norwegian woman from Adwick-le-Street (p. 71).

However, it is important not to confuse race and identity, by talking of 'Viking blood' or 'Viking genes'. Our genes determine neither the language we speak nor the clothes we wear, and cultural factors are just as important as DNA in determining who we are. We are also acutely aware of the dangers of developing attitudes based on biological race. Modern archaeologists and historians have adopted the term ethnicity to indicate identity which is cultural rather than racial.

Jacquetta Hawkes famously wrote that 'Every age gets the Stonehenge it deserves', by which she meant that Stonehenge has been a Druid temple, a landing site for flying saucers, or an astronomical calendar, according to the interests of the times. The same could be said about our stories about Vikings, and they have been alternately, noble savages, raiders, marauders and rapists, peaceful traders, entrepreneurs, explorers, early democrats, or

IKEA sales personnel, according to what we want them to be. This small volume has attempted to use recent archaeological research to introduce what is important to know about the peoples who inhabited Scandinavia in the 9th to 11th centuries and to trace those expansions which brought them into contact with other early medieval societies. It has explored how the term Viking came to be applied to them, and examined how they have been reinvented many times, from the Icelandic Sagas to 21st-century heritage attractions.

In each of the situations in which we encounter Scandinavian settlers their Viking identity is rather different, and nowhere is it unmodified. A Scandinavian settler in early 10th-century Northumbria may have retained the Norse tongue, but with various English borrowings. When he went to the growing urban market in Jorvik he would have seen new cellared and plank-built workshops, unlike the old Anglo-Saxon or Danish houses. In Jorvik he may have bought new brooches for his new English wife, neither in the style her mother wore, nor like those worn by the women back home, but in a hybrid form, reflecting elements of both fashions. When he died, if he were wealthy, he might expect to have a stone memorial erected over his grave, not like the grave of his father, nor like the graves of the English. If study of the Vikings has a contemporary message for us it is that identity is not an immutable concept. Further research should continue to help elucidate the circumstances in which new identities are formed and the ways in which they are expressed, not just for Vikings, but for all societies.

Timeline

	700	800	900	1000	1100	1200	1300	1400

SCANDINAVIA

- c.704–10 Ribe founded
- Coins minted at Ribe
- c.900 Århus founded
- 948 Bishops appointed to Hedeby, Ribe and Århus
- 726 Kanhave canal constructed
- c.965 Harald Bluetooth converted to Christianity
- 737 Danevirke first phase
- c.980 Construction of the Trelleborg fortresses
- 1027 First stone church at Roskilde
- c.750 Birka founded
- c.995 Coin minting at Sigtuna
- 808 Reric destroyed and Hedeby founded
- 1070s Skuldelev ships scuttled
- 820s Ansgar's first
- c.980 Hedeby 1 built
- missionary journeys
- 834 Oseberg ship burial
- c.880s Haraldr Finehair attempts to unite Norway
- 995 Olaf Tryggvason unites Norway
- c.990s Trondheim founded
- 1050 Coins minted at Trondheim

CONTINENTAL EUROPE

- 800 Coronation of the Emperor Charlemagne
- 799 First Viking raids on Frankia
- 834–7 Annual raids on Dorestad
- 852 Viking fleet on Seine
- 911 Foundation of Normandy by Rollo
- 930s Vikings expelled from Brittany

	700	800	900	1000	1100	1200	1300	1400
EASTERN EUROPE	737 Danekirve first phase		c.862 Rurik, ruler of Novgorod 882 Kiev founded c.910–2 Viking fleet on Caspian Sea	980s Conversion of Russia	c.1040 Ingvar's expedition to the east			
BRITISH ISLES		790s First Viking raids	860s Intensive Viking activity in England 867 Danish capture of York 870s Vikings settle in England 871–99 Alfred, King of Wessex c.870 Establishment of earldom of Orkney 841 Longphort established at Dublin 902 Vikings expelled from Dublin	950s Intensive raiding on Wales 954 Erik Bloodaxe expelled from York 991 Battle of Maldon 1016–35 Cnut, King of England	1066 Battle of Stamford Bridge 1117 Magnus martyred on Egilsay 1160s Norman conquest of Ireland			
NORTH ATLANTIC		c.800 Irish hermits in the Faroes and Iceland c.860 Norse settlement on the Faroes c.870–930 Norse settlement of Iceland	930 Foundation of the Icelandic Althing	c.1000 Iceland converted to Christianity		Icelandic Sagas		
GREENLAND AND NORTH AMERICA				c.985 Erik the Red settles in Greenland c.1000 Voyages to Vinland	c.1125 Bishopric at Gardar		c.1350 West settlement abandoned	c.1450 East settlement abandoned

Further reading

For a non-literate society Vikings are good booksellers. There is a huge number of general books, many lavishly illustrated. I have largely avoided listing these, and have preferred instead to cite edited volumes of papers in English, many of which also provide accessible introductions to Scandinavian material. Most of these also have full bibliographies to other sources and primary evidence. Because of the rapid growth of new archaeological discoveries I have also emphasized recent works and generally avoided works more than 15 years old.

General introductions

J. Graham-Campbell (ed.), *Cultural Atlas of the Viking World* (Andromeda, 1994)

J. Hines, A. Lane, and M. Redknap (eds), *Land, Sea and Home* (Maney, 2004)

J. Jesch, *Women in the Viking Age* (Boydell & Brewer, 1991)

P. Sawyer (ed.), *The Oxford Illustrated History of the Vikings* (Oxford University Press, 1997)

Scandinavia

E. Christiansen, *The Norsemen in the Viking Age* (Blackwell, 2002)

E. Roesdahl, *Viking Age Denmark* (British Museum Publications, 1982)

J. Adams and K. Holman (eds), *Scandinavia and Europe 800–1350: Contact, Conflict and Coexistence* (Brepols 2004)

Religion

N. Price, *The Viking Way* (Dept of Archaeology and Ancient History, Uppsala, 2002)

Ships

O. Crumlin-Pedersen and B. Munch Thye (eds), *The Ship as Symbol in Prehistoric and Medieval Scandinavia* (The National Museum [Copenhagen], 1995)

A. Nørgård Jørgensen *et al.* (eds), *Maritime Warfare in Northern Europe* (The National Museum [Copenhagen], 2002)

Vikings in Literature and Runes

R. I. Page, *Chronicles of the Vikings* (British Museum Press, 1995)

B. Sawyer, *The Viking-Age Rune-Stones* (Oxford University Press, 2000)

England and Wales

D. M. Hadley and J. D. Richards (eds), *Cultures in Contact: Scandinavian Settlement in England in the Ninth and Tenth Centuries* (Brepols, 2000)

R. A. Hall *et al.*, *Aspects of Anglo-Scandinavian York* (Council for British Archaeology, The Archaeology of York 8/4, 2004)

J. D. Richards, *Viking Age England* (new edn, Tempus, 2004)

J. Graham-Campbell, R. Hall, J. Jesch, and D. N. Parsons (eds), *Vikings and the Danelaw* (Oxbow Books, 2001)

M. Redknap, *Vikings in Wales: An Archaeological Quest* (National Museums & Galleries of Wales, 2000)

Scotland

J. Graham-Campbell and C. Batey, *Vikings in Scotland: An Archaeological Survey* (Edinburgh University Press, 1998)

A. Ritchie, *Viking Scotland* (Batsford, 1993)

Ireland

H. B. Clarke, M. Ní Mhaonaigh, and R. Ó Floinn (eds), *Ireland and Scandinavia in the Early Viking Age* (Four Courts Press, 1998)

A.-C. Larsen (ed.), *The Vikings in Ireland* (Viking Ship Museum, 2001)

The North Atlantic

J. H. Barrett (ed.), *Contact, Continuity, and Collapse: The Norse Colonization of the North Atlantic* (Brepols, 2003)

C. E. Batey, J. Jesch, and C. D. Morris (eds), *The Viking Age in Caithness, Orkney and the North Atlantic* (Edinburgh University Press, 1993)

W. W. Fitzhugh and E. I. Ward (eds), *Vikings: The North Atlantic Saga* (Smithsonian Institution Press, 2000)

S. Lewis-Simpson (ed.), *Vinland Revisited: The Norse World at the Turn of the First Millennium* (Historic Sites Association, 2004)

Reinventing the Vikings

A. Wawn, *The Vikings and the Victorians: Inventing the Old North in 19th-Century Britain* (D. S. Brewer, 2000)

Index

Index

Index

Visit the
VERY SHORT
INTRODUCTIONS
Web site

www.oup.co.uk/vsi

➤ **Information** about all published titles

➤ News of **forthcoming books**

➤ **Extracts** from the books, including titles
not yet published

➤ **Reviews** and views

➤ **Links** to other **web sites** and main
OUP web page

➤ Information about **VSIs in translation**

➤ **Contact** the editors

➤ **Order** other **VSIs** on-line

Expand your collection of
VERY SHORT INTRODUCTIONS

THE ANGLO-SAXON AGE

A Very Short Introduction

John Blair

First published as part of the best-selling *Oxford Illustrated History of Britain*, John Blair's Very Short Introduction to the Ango-Saxon Age covers the period from the earliest English settlements to the Norman victory in 1066. This book is a brief introduction to the political, social, religious, and cultural history of an age when so many basic aspects of modern England were formed: its language, governmental institutions, rural landscape, communications, and towns.

www.oup.co.uk/isbn/0-19-285403-8

ARCHAEOLOGY
A Very Short Introduction
Paul Bahn

This entertaining Very Short Introduction reflects the
enduring popularity of archaeology – a subject which
appeals as a pastime, career, and academic discipline,
encompasses the whole globe, and surveys 2.5 million
years. From deserts to jungles, from deep caves to
mountain tops, from pebble tools to satellite photo-
graphs, from excavation to abstract theory, archaeology
interacts with nearly every other discipline in its attempts
to reconstruct the past.

'very lively indeed and remarkably perceptive ... a quite
brilliant and level-headed look at the curious world of
archaeology'

Barry Cunliffe, University of Oxford

'It is often said that well-written books are rare in archaeology, but this is a model of good writing for a general
audience. The book is full of jokes, but its serious
message – that archaeology can be a rich and fascinat-
ing subject – it gets across with more panache than any
other book I know.'

Simon Denison, editor of *British Archaeology*

www.oup.co.uk/vsi/archaeology

VERY SHORT INTRODUCTIONS

Derived from the best-selling *Oxford Illustrated History of Britain*, the following British history titles are now available in the Very Short Introductions series:

➤ **Roman Britain**
Peter Salway

➤ **The Anglo-Saxon Age**
John Blair

➤ **Medieval Britain**
John Gillingham & Ralph A. Griffiths

➤ **The Tudors**
John Guy

➤ **Stuart Britain**
John Morrill

➤ **Eighteenth-Century Britain**
Paul Langford

➤ **Nineteenth-Century Britain**
Christopher Harvie & H. C. G. Matthew

➤ **Twentieth-Century Britain**
Kenneth Morgan